D1488160

A$$ HOLE

ALSO BY MARTIN KIHN

House of Lies

A$$ HOLE

How I Got Rich & Happy by Not Giving a Damn About Anyone & How You Can, Too

Martin Kihn

BROADWAY BOOKS   NEW YORK

PUBLISHED BY BROADWAY BOOKS

Copyright © 2008 by Martin Kihn

All Rights Reserved

Published in the United States by Broadway Books, an imprint
of The Doubleday Broadway Publishing Group, a division of
Random House, Inc., New York.
www.broadwaybooks.com

BROADWAY BOOKS and its logo, a letter B bisected on the diagonal,
are trademarks of Random House, Inc.

Book design by Ellen Cipriano

Library of Congress Cataloging-in-Publication Data
Kihn, Martin.
    Asshole : how I got rich & happy by not giving a damn about anyone
& how you can, too / Martin Kihn.
        p. cm.
    1. Conduct of life—Humor. 2. Selfishness—Humor. I. Title.

PN6231.C6142K54 2008
818'.602—dc22

                                                    2007045339
    ISBN 978-0-7679-2726-0

PRINTED IN THE UNITED STATES OF AMERICA

10 9 8 7 6 5 4 3 2 1

First Edition

For my parents,
who did not raise an asshole;
and for my wife,
who had to live with one.

Author's Note

A$$hole is based on an experiment I conducted on my real life. In order to protect unwitting co-workers, innocent family members, and others, I have made a number of changes to what really happened. I have altered most names and physical characteristics, created composite characters and combined events, and reimagined some scenes to make them funnier.

If that makes me an asshole, then thank you.

A$$ ◎ HOLE

INTRODUCTION

I was the nicest guy in the world—and it was killing me.

This is not just chin music. If you'd asked anyone who knew me then—before my glorious rebirth as an Asshole—who was the nicest guy in the world, you'd get one of two answers. Either they'd say my name immediately, or they'd say some other name, then go, "Oh, wait, I forgot about Marty—*he's* the nicest guy in the world."

My life was a dictionary without the word "no." Years passed in elaborate acrobatic contortions getting out of everybody's way.

Except my own.

Here's the kind of guy that I was: If you asked me to do you a favor—even the kind of favor that required me to go so far out of my way I needed a map, a translator, and an oxygen tank, even if I didn't know you that well, I might hesitate a second, hoping you'd think of someone else to irritate. But I'd always say "Yes!"

That's not true. If I really didn't want to do it, I'd say something different. Something like "You bet!"

I seemed to spend my whole life giving money to anyone who asked (even rich people, like the Metropolitan Opera), doing websites for free, walking other people's dogs, bringing back to the office complicated lunch orders of some cuisine I don't even like (say, Chinese), and then, upon learning the place had messed up one of the orders, *going back out* to get the right thing.

I was a telemarketer's dream. The kind of guy who agreed to buy not only the Identity Theft Solution, but also the high-rate home equity loan, just to get you off the phone.

I was a man who always backed down in a fight—who didn't even get into the fight in the first place, because to have a fight assumes you have a point of view. A man who'd managed to turn an almost embarrassingly rich portfolio of advantages earlier in life into a crappy apartment in the middle of a barrio; a net worth more negative than my philosophy; a pet who laughed at my commands; and a job where I was about to become the guy who didn't get promoted because he lacked the eye of the tiger, the mojo, or even the desire to be in that stupid job in the first place.

Oh, and I was about to turn forty.

But believe it or not, this is a tale of hope and redemption. This is my story of glory.

It begins on that birthday, a day not much worse than my usual at that time, and no better. I was myself; I was nice. Nothing special. That morning, something in me snapped.

I made a decision to take a stand against my weaknesses and fears and actively question my philosophy of life. It's better to give than receive? Then take *this*!

Why can't we all just get along? Because we *can't*.

It's nice to be important, but it's more important to be nice. On what *planet*?

I made the radical decision to whittle and chop and burn away the defects that would toss me into an early grave—defects like consideration, politeness, giving a fuck what you think—to blowtorch away my old personality and uncover the rock-hard warrior (and abs) within. I would learn from the masters, the legendary bastards and bitches who had walked before me, like Donald Trump, Scarface, and that guy in my building with the tattoo on his face. I'd study the works of the great fuck-you philosophers from Nietzsche to Dogbert. I'd do the things assholes do like kickboxing, attending NRA conventions, driving fast on the shoulder of the road, using the speakerphone for long meetings, screaming at co-workers for no reason, blaming the waiter for things the chef did, returning items with no receipt not because I don't have the receipt but because I can't be bothered to look for it, asking people I barely know for favors, cutting in line, eating garlic bagels on the subway, complaining, complaining, complaining.

There would be me and my needs. And then there would be me and my needs. Any questions?

I'd had it. America is not a country for the nice. Not anymore, if it ever was. No, America is a country for the prick. The bullshit artist and his coterie. The screaming diva. My intention was not to become a sadist; I didn't have it in me. My intention was simply to do what it takes to win, baby—even if what it takes is to turn one hundred eighty pounds of puff pastry into a Grade A bag of dicks with an expense account.

So I set out on a program of self-realization, learning how to remake myself into an Asshole. It was a voyage of many months and thousands of dollars, and it succeeded beyond my wildest dreams, as you will see. I lay it out here step by step so that you, too, can follow in my path.

Having taken this journey before you, I can honestly say that it's worth it. You may never be as rich and good-looking as I am, but don't let that discourage you. Even I could be richer and better looking, although that would be cruel.

So how, you ask, can you put this program to work in your life?

Here's how: *Put it to work!* Get out there. Make that big world your bitch. Whatever you decide to do, it is most important that you do *something*.

Because the alternative is to keep doing what you're doing and keep getting what you've got.

Believe me, that is definitely not what your spouse wants.

RULE$ OF THE GAME

I was about to jump into a program that could be life-threatening, and I wondered if I really wanted to have *no rules*. Would I suddenly inhabit a world where, say, shop-lifting was fine as long as I didn't get caught? Where I could "dine 'n' dash" and dance naked in the streets just because—well, just because I wanted to? Did not that way lie chaos, confusion, and those baggy orange jumpsuits?

I decided: Yes. I would need some rules—the bare minimum necessary to keep me sane yet provide total freedom to become an Asshole.

After some deliberation, these were the ones I settled on:

THE RULES: THINGS I WOULD NOT DO

1. **Any felony**—including murder, rape, arson, arms trafficking, and traitorous thoughts
2. **Substance use**—illegal and, at my age, kind of sad
3. **Surgery**—plastic, brain, or otherwise
4. **Parenting**—either natural, via intensive communion with my wife, or adoptive; my thinking here was, what kind of a kid would want an Asshole for a parent?
5. **Cheating on wife**—a survival instinct on my part: She is very perceptive, holds a grudge, has a Welsh temper, and, since she recently enrolled in culinary school, has a large collection of Teutonic knives she keeps so sharp I get a nosebleed just thinking about them. Also, I love her.
6. **Smiling**—except when other people are in pain (a tactic of psychological warfare)
7. **Following rules**

I thought of other no-nos—like tipping, doing favors, paying retail—but I was wary of anything too prescriptive. I was becoming a victim of rule creep, which would violate my own Rule #7.

Okay, now that we have our guidelines, there's one more hurdle we need to clear before we can begin.

Commitment to any program as demanding as mine requires the conviction that you will realize the life you want. Take it from me, you will not be able to meet the harsh rigors of this life-changing regimen unless you're as wide awake as I was to your many, many shortcomings.

So take a moment to complete the following self-assessment. This should make you feel bad enough about yourself that you'll be ready to get moving.

SELF-QUIZ:
DO YOU NEED THIS PROGRAM?

Answer the following Yes or No questions, selecting the option that best describes what you *normally* do or think in the given situation. Don't answer as the person you wish you were; answer as the person that you are, no matter how lonely and fat that makes you feel.

Select only one answer (Y/N) to each question. There is no (M)aybe anymore.

1. Do you feel you can never be happy if somebody, somewhere is sad?
2. When you get the wrong dish in a restaurant, do you just assume you ordered wrong?
3. Have you ever stayed up all night worried you've offended someone?
4. When you apologized, did that person have no clue what you were talking about?
5. Do you believe that plants have feelings?
6. When you enter a room, do people start napping?
7. Did you pay the manufacturer's suggested retail price (MSRP) for your car?
8. When you "fly off the handle," does nobody seem to notice?

9. Does it make you proud when someone takes credit for your work?
10. Do your co-workers seem to have trouble remembering your name?
11. Have you ever been invited to "girls' night out," even though you're a man?
12. Did you go?

Scoring: For every No answer give yourself +1 point; for Yes give yourself -1 point. Sum up your total point score. Now find a piece of plain white paper, preferably 8½" x 11", and a black felt-tip pen or marker. Write down your point total in large block numbers directly in the center of the piece of paper. Fold the paper so the shorter (i.e., 8½") ends meet. Now rotate the page 90 degrees and fold it again. Keep rotating and folding the paper until you have completed this action five (5) times. You should now have a very compact, accordion-like wad of white paper that is very difficult to fold anymore.

Now take this wad of paper and shove it where the sun don't shine.

Done? Good.

My point is this: Of *course* you need this book. As with alcoholism, gambling, and over-loving the fried foods, even *suspecting* you have a problem like niceness all but guarantees that you in fact do have the problem. So stop musing and start moving.

THE TEN STEPS OF ASSHOLISM

Change doesn't happen overnight. People like us have spent decades being considerate and thoughtful—bad qualities that can't be erased in an instant. Through hard trial and error, I have developed an effective program of Assholism: Ten Steps toward your awakening as a prick. The following chapters describe my own experience with the Steps, and indicate how you can apply my insights to your own so-called life.

These Steps are:

PREPARATION: *Set Your Butt on Fire*
- Looking closely at your sorry-assed self and becoming afraid—very afraid

STEP #1: *Keep Your Eye on the (Ass)Hole, Not the Donut*
- Finding role models and badly dressed heroes who do Asshole right

STEP #2: *Get a Life (Coach)*
- Locating the right professionals to help kick-start your program

STEP #3: *Act As If*
- Pretending you're a dick—and, like, totally loving it

STEP #4: *Think Win-Lose*
- Getting over yourself, so you can get over on others

STEP #5: *Practice Practice Practice*
- Trying out your new offensive skills on an unprepared public

STEP #6: *Be a Fighter, Not a Lover*
- Honing your body into a lean, walking sphincter through the use of pain and caffeine

STEP #7: *Become the Alpha Dog*
- Getting into the simple, Asshole-like mindset of your four-legged enemy

STEP #8: *Put the "Tame" Back in "Team"*
- Applying your new skills to sow dread and confusion in the office

STEP #9: *Never Surrender*
- Realizing there are no obstacles, only schmucks who desperately deserve a beat-down

STEP #10: *Life Is a Gift, So Return It*
- Finding out that the end is never as clean as we thought

PREPAR
ATION

Set Your
Butt on Fire

"It is necessary . . . to learn to be able not to be good."

—Niccolò Machiavelli,
The Prince

The first step in any journey is not to decide where you're going—it's to get out of bed. You need to look around and see where you're starting. If you're like me—and I'm sorry, you are—this will be a painful process. You will be pecked at by could-haves and should-haves. But even worse is the prospect of staying in place. You've been burned your whole life. Now it's time to set your butt on fire.

It was the day I turned forty that I decided to change my life, not in the usual way, by buying a sports car and getting rejected by younger women in bars. No, I decided to transform myself by doing whatever it took to become a total Asshole.

Now, I wasn't particularly upset about turning forty, confronting middle age, facing the inevitable disappointments and failures. I'd felt middle-aged since that day in my twenties when a (slightly) younger person tried to pass by me in the aisle of an airplane when we were deplaning and said, "Excuse me, sir."

Sir?! From that moment, I'd felt kind of old. And my looks backed me up.

Considered fairly handsome in a Midwestern mode, I was routinely taken to be older than my years. I blamed my diet (execrable), my exercise regimen (hah), my city (Manhattan), and my being too nice. How this last part had anything to do with my appearance I was not exactly clear, but I was pretty sure being too nice had ruined every aspect of my life and so was perfectly capable of making me ugly.

So I woke up on this special day in the usual way: whacked on the jaw by a two-by-four with nails sticking out of it.

At least, that's what it felt like. In fact it was my darling doggie, Hola, welcoming me to a brand new day on spaceship earth. Because I hesitated a moment getting up, Hola jumped up on my chest and started using my head as a speed bag, doing her reps.

With another dog, this might be cute. With Hola it was actually dangerous. She is a four-year-old Bernese Mountain Dog and weighs over ninety pounds—in fact, since she's extorting more food out of me every day, she's probably closer to one hundred, which is getting into International Boxing Federation flyweight territory.

"Hola, down," I said, halfheartedly.

In the old Soviet Union, there was a saying, "We pretend to work, and they pretend to pay us." That's the way it was with my four-legged love child and me. I pretended to give her commands, and she pretended to obey me. Should she be up on the bed, uninvited? Probably not. Should she be hammering my aging puss like it was a home improvement project? I don't think so. But what was I gonna do about it, exactly? Put her on warning?

I ducked away from her while she was momentarily distracted by chewing up my pillow, and escaped to wipe the saliva off my face and review the to-do list for the day. Let's see, there was being walked by my dog, standing squashed in a train for an hour, running to the office too late for breakfast, getting besieged and second-guessed at work, receiving another iffy performance review, saying yes to some as-yet-unidentified users, and coming home to a woman who once told me she loved me despite the fact that I was never going to make any money. Happy birthday, Marty.

"Hola!"

I bribed her away from my pillow with some high-end cheese from Citarella. She had migrated us up the scale, from Velveeta to Kraft to Cracker Barrel to cheese-store cheddar to the very finest imported cheeses of the world. How she did this, I'm not sure. Just as I'm unsure how we used to get away with feeding her the food other dogs eat but now had to special order super-expensive prescription-only food from a veterinarian in Westchester County. We didn't even live in Westchester County.

"Hola, sit!"

She smirked as she stood there. Then she tapped my leg with her forepaw, the universal request for Danish Beemster Extra Aged Gouda, on a little cracker.

After I'd lured her into her harness, she pulled me through the door and over to my neighbor Ramón's. Ramón is a slick-looking lawyer about my age who lives in a much bigger apartment on my floor with a view of the Hudson River. My apartment has a view of the Hudson Airshaft.

Ramón barely acknowledged me—he was on his cell phone, doing a deal—as he ordered his German Shepherd, Misty, out of the apartment and shut the door behind her. The thing about Misty was she was beautifully behaved—the epitome of sterling dog manners—but only when Ramón was around. With me, she was a terrorist in training.

I knew what was coming. Misty gave Hola a little good-morning kiss, girlfriend-to-girlfriend, and then the two of them glared up at me and growled.

"It's my birthday," I said, hoping for mercy.

They ran for the elevator, dragging me behind them.

Between the two of them, they outmuscled me, and the sight of me getting yanked around my block by these canines like some demented water-skier probably provided hours of great material to local comedians. If I spoke Spanish, I'd laugh along with them.

As it was, I was wondering—hurtling through the air, as my personal wolf pack hunted down and cornered a Big Mac wrapper—how it was I'd agreed to walk Misty in the first place. Hola, I understood. She was my wife's dog, and I lived with my wife, and my wife was unacquainted with the dawn. That I got. But this asshole neighbor's clawed menace to society? Every day? For free? I remembered Ramón saying something like "You're going out anyway, right?" and that making some kind of sense . . . but everything made sense to me. That was the problem. I saw sides to issues that weren't even there. It was like I lived in an eleven-dimensional universe.

After I dropped Misty off—Ramón was still on the phone—

I fed Hola her million-dollar meal, gave her a little extra water for the day, and got ready. I took a look around my castle. It was dark. Two tiny bedrooms in a co-op so far up on the West Side it wasn't even Harlem anymore, it was Upstate Manhattan. My goal when I was younger had always been to own an apartment in Manhattan, and so I did, I suppose. I should have been more specific with my dreams.

Oh, and the building's elevators, which were designed during the Truman Administration and were apparently outfitted with noisemakers not long after, ran directly past our bedroom. Up and down, 24/7. But it wasn't so bad—eventually, we'd get so deaf it wouldn't even bother us.

I took a deep breath and kissed my wife, Gloria, goodbye. She was a slender sleeping beauty with thick red hair and flawless skin. In my case, my better half certainly is; and there are those, like my mother, who wonder out loud how I got so lucky. I claim that when we met, in the 1990's, being super-nice was not such a deal-breaker.

A few months older than I was, she looked much younger, but I didn't hold this against her. It was better than the alternative. She was known for her tender wit and extremely good nature, which had somehow survived fifteen years in Manhattan intact. As naturally gregarious as I was self-conscious, she made friends so easily it was almost offensive. What she continued to see in me, I was not quite sure.

"Happy birthday," she whispered, smiling up at me.

"I hope so," I said, and took a deep breath, stood up straight, headed for the door with a can-do attitude, and tripped on one of Hola's squeaky toys. Hola thought this was very funny.

"Go get 'em!" said Gloria, who was not, it seemed, too sleepy to do what she does best: lift me up.

"Okay," I said.

Okay.

The only thing wrong with my neighborhood was that it was where I lived. Other than that I had no complaint. My Dominican neighbors really were very lovely people, with large rambunctious families and little pets that made nice bite-size snacks for Hola, and good attitudes about America. I had almost nothing they had, except love handles, and debt.

On my way to the No. 1 train that morning, I ran into Ramón coming out of Twin Donut.

"Hola," I said.

He ignored me.

I dreaded Twin Donut. Every morning at exactly the same moment I appeared with exactly the same order—every morning—and I had yet to receive the same thing twice. If you locked a combinatorial mathematics convention in a room they could not come up with as many variations on a large coffee with no sugar and a corn muffin as I had received in my bag.

I'd had the same server, every morning, for two solid years. And always the guy looked at me like he'd never seen me before in his life. When he looked at me at all.

"Large no sugar corn muffin," I said.

"How many sugars?"

"No sugar."

"Two sugars," he said, about to ladle them in.

"No sugar."

"Glazed cruller," he said, sacking one up.

"Corn muffin."

"Two crullers."

And this was a good day. Often I would come in and the guy would completely ignore me, holding a kind of tree-worshipping session with his mop. This guy was always multitasking, baking donuts while manning the register while also mopping, which was made more difficult by the fact that his mop had no water in it. It was not a dry mop, just a wet mop in the midst of a dry spell. It's not like he worked alone, either. There were three other fellows farther down the counter, holding a deep personal discussion about, I think, titties.

On the train, the coffee always tasted sweet. I suspected he prepared the cup for me ahead of time, howling with laughter.

I was living in this neighborhood because it was the only place in Manhattan where I could afford to buy an apartment that my wife felt was large enough for her naps.

I'd moved to Manhattan almost twenty years before, during the era of New Wave, when people still actually got mugged, and were afraid, and when Greenwich Village was full of gay men and Chelsea was kind of seedy and you didn't need three generations of inherited wealth to be able to buy a one-bedroom somewhere south of Massachusetts.

As my friends Ben and Brad kept reminding me, as we all bravely marched out of our thirties, at least we had our health. Actually, Ben had a skin rash and Brad looked like a warm bowl of death, but I got their point.

On the subway I ran into Ramón again, but he was much too important to chat.

"You," he said, looking down at his PDA.

"Hola, again."

"Heh."

"Had a good walk with Misty this morning."

"Not what she tells me."

Although we got on at the same stop, at the same moment, he had somehow procured a seat and I was left to stand. I can't remember ever sitting in the New York City subway system. Maybe once or twice, in the early '90s, but I might have dreamed it. Ramón had done better than just get a seat: He'd acquired one seat with an option on another one. The option was held by his computer bag and his attitude.

A half hour later, as we were pulling into Times Square, I glanced at the screen of the PDA he'd been ferociously pounding on during the entire trip—so busy he couldn't talk—and I saw he had been playing Minesweeper.

"Adios," I said to him, and he pushed past me so hard I spilled some of my sweet, cold coffee on my shirt.

"Shit!"

An old lady next to me—who'd seen what had happened—smiled at me.

"Get over it," she said, kicking me out of her way.

In those days my days had no highlights, but I did very much look forward to getting off the train. But not today. Why? Because I was going in for my annual bitch slap and plea for atonement. The technical name for this was performance review.

To postpone this incredible pleasure, I stopped off at Duane Reade to get a box of Kleenex tissues, the kind with aloe vera. It wasn't for me, but I'll get there.

I worked in advertising. My sacred mission in life was to pile more debt onto people who could ill afford it by selling them credit cards they didn't need. Because most of these people were not quite as stupid as they looked, my job was to pretend we were actually selling them things like "security" and "free-dom" when in fact we were more likely driving them to an early grave.

The joy of my working environment was compounded by the fact that, although I was the lowest possible level of vice president in an office teeming with low-level vice presidents, I was one of the oldest.

"Hey, chief," said my office-mate, when I arrived.

Despite being a vice president, I shared an office. A small one. And though my office-mate was pleasant enough, and quiet, he liked to sit in the dark. "It helps me think," I believe he told me once. So to facilitate his idea quest we sat in perpetual twilight, with no window.

Two of my colleagues came in, young women who often worked for me. I'll call them Emily and Eleanor because those are their names. They were both attractive, although I was getting to the age when almost any woman under thirty made me feel like a pedophile. I don't remember young women being that cute ten years ago. My standards had slipped.

Emily was the taller and more emotional of the two, bone-thin with Bozo-like hair and a pierced tongue. Eleanor was very serious, conservative in all things but politics, chalk white with a blunt-cut blond topiary. She played bass in a band called Sexual Side Effects. Without saying a word, I handed Emily the box of Kleenex. I did this because, as usual, she was crying.

"Th-thanks," she sobbed.

Before I could ask her what was wrong, the phone rang. I knew what it was.

The bitch slap.

I gathered up my notebook and pen, and my breath, said goodbye to the girls, and headed off to the boss's office for my appraisal. But before I got there I passed by a young man I'll call the Nemesis. He was an extraordinarily bulked-up guy, dark-skinned and gorgeous with fierce blue eyes, his thick black hair tied back in a marketing-issue ponytail. Rumor had it he was half-Cherokee, owned a horse ranch out West, and was ex–Special Forces.

This charmer was poking his finger into the chest of a kid who worked for him, saying savagely, "I need you to buy a clue, Todd, 'cause the work you're doing here blows chunks. Don't make me take you down."

Ch-choking out an apology, the offender—who I knew to be exceptionally smart, and a tireless worker—slunk off.

The Nemesis turned to me and beamed. "Whassup?"

"Ah, you know—"

"That bad, huh? You look kind of down. Like you're going to your funeral or something, hah hah."

"Actually, I am."

"Oh," he said, nodding. "Performance review. Good luck man. From what I hear, you're gonna need it, hah hah."

"You had yours yet?"

"Oh, yeah. It went super-great. Just radical. They're talking about—well, I don't want to jinx it."

"What?"

He lowered his voice, which was outrageously loud to begin with, to a level just below a scream. His version of whispering. "*The p-word*," he said.

"What p-word?" I was thinking: *penalty, purgatory, pecker-wood . . .*

"Promotion."

"What'd they say?"

" 'We can't make any promises till we've done the budgets,'

and blah blah blah—you know, the usual shit that happens every time you get promoted."

I wouldn't know.

"Anyway, listen—when you're done, drop by my office, we need to talk. About Lucifer."

Lucifer was a potential project I was attached to and the Nemesis was openly trying to pry it out of my cold, dead hands, and I didn't feel like talking about it with him, not later, not after that, not ever.

"Sure thing," I smiled, and headed off to face my fate.

The Nemesis was an outside consultant, and I'd never been allowed to see his résumé. Maybe it was classified. If you'd asked me what my major problems with the Nemesis were, as I knocked on my boss's door that morning and said my quiet prayers, I'd have told you there were two big ones.

First, he was a lying belligerent dickhead who enjoyed berating underlings, especially in front of their peers, and would kick his cousin's corpse in the street if he thought it would make him a dollar. And second—much, much worse—he was ten years younger than me.

"Come in," said my boss.

"Hiya."

"Have a seat. Let's get this over with."

It was just the two of us, and my boss is a friendly sort of woman, so I was surprised to find the air so oddly charged. I felt like security was right outside the door, waiting for the signal.

"Running late today?" she said. There were pages on the desk in front of her, and she spread them apart. "Where to begin? How are you?"

"Okay."

"You tired? You look tired."

"People always say that. I think it's my diet—"

"So how do you feel the year went?"

That was it for the small talk. She was a fabulously tall African-American woman with tight curls and a pair of those bold square-framed glasses they issue along with marketing degrees at prestigious Midwestern universities. She also had a huge warm personality that she was at this moment storing in a box under her desk.

"Pretty good, I guess. I've been working on—"

"You sure about that? You're feeling *good*?"

"Well . . . I've . . . I mean—"

"We've got some issues. Let's get into the substance, okay?"

I felt something drop. The window behind her back showed me that the sky was dark, and the line of exotic tequila bottles lined up on top of her sparsely populated bookshelf looked like an army of deliverance.

"Wha—what issues?"

"Let me tell you a story," she started. I hated this: people telling stories that started with, "Let me tell you a story." It was a polite way of saying, "Now shut up."

"So," she started, "when I started out I did a lot of job hopping. Two years here, two years there. Mostly in public relations, yuck. It's okay—when you're young, there's a lot you don't know about working and there shouldn't be a stigma to it, right? But at a certain point I found the consulting world, like you did, and then here, at the agency, and I made a move from the kind of work I was doing before—execution type stuff—into what VPs are supposed to do. You know what that is?"

"I'm . . . I . . ."

"See—that's interesting." She picked up a couple of sheets of paper, glanced down at them, put them back on the desk, and

all the time she looked sort of disgusted, like her feet were hurting her. I didn't know where she was going.

"I'm sorry," I said.

"Selling. That's what VPs do, Marty. They're out there, they
hustle, they're over at the client site, talking to the decision-
makers, selling in the work. Keeps the engine going, and it's
what you're *supposed* to be doing. Get it?"

I nodded, and she tapped the papers, which contained the
detailed bullet-pointed list of my personal failures, which I
would be required to read closely, take into my soul, and sign.
But that was later. Right now, she said:

"There're two big points in here I got from talking to the
people you work with. Number one, you're the nicest guy in the
world—"

"Thank you—"

"—let me finish. It's not all good. See, everybody likes to
work with you, but that's kind of irrelevant, where I sit. If you
don't get that edge, there's no work for them to work on. See
what I mean? You gotta kick butt. Avenue A's out there, Digitas
is out there"—she named some of our top competitors—"and
they're killing on your accounts. They're eating our brunch.
You're not pushy enough. You gotta get in there, close the deal,
understand?"

I swallowed. My throat was dry.

"Take"—she named the Nemesis, as I knew she would—
"He's out there every day, taking no prisoners. Digitas is afraid of
him. Avenue A sees him coming down the hall, they run for
cover."

Frankly, I thought, anyone who sees him coming down the
hall runs for cover, including his own mother.

"*That's* what we need you to do," she continued. "Think you can? 'Cause I'm not so sure. It might be this place isn't right for you. Maybe you're just too nice for corporate life. Ever thought of that? That's okay. It's okay to be who you are. What I'm seeing now is a bad fit. And I'm going to have to make a promotion decision soon. Any thoughts?"

I focused on breathing, in and out. Among my many flaws was a tendency to be oversensitive, so I was trying not to react in a dramatic way. Say, by bursting into tears. I could deal with this.

"Well . . ."

And then, my life changed. This is how.

There are times when people say things to us, ordinary things, and we're ready to hear them, and we *do*.

What my boss said was this:

"You've got two choices here, Marty. I like you—I really do—so it's okay with me which one you pick. Number one is you can be who you are, and find another job somewhere, maybe working in a library or something, hah hah. And number two is you can be more like [the Nemesis]."

"People loathe him," I said.

"He's effective. And *that*," she said, standing up to indicate this meeting was now over, "is all that really counts."

"That's it?"

"Bottom line is there's only budget to promote one of you. It's him or you." She let that sentence hang there: *It's him or you.* Not much wiggle room there. "Right now we haven't made up our minds—but you can see the way the wind's blowing?"

The wind was apparently blowing right out the Nemesis's ass at me. I nodded.

"Okay, then. Now I've got to take this—"

When I got back to my office, incredibly, Emily was still

there, still crying. I asked her if I could borrow one of her Kleenex. She took one look at me and handed me the box.

How did this discussion with my boss change my life?

It didn't happen right away. Change is slow. Real change is so slow it seems not to happen at all. And then everything's different, and you wonder how.

I had one personal day left, and there were no clients to hit up for work since I was so ineffective, so I left the office and got a double cheeseburger from Kosmo's Diner and went to my favorite spot at the fence by the Chelsea dog run, and ate my cheeseburger and watched the dogs.

I thought about what my boss had said. Was she right about me?

In the park, there was the usual contingent of gorgeous, exotic purebred dogs, like Siberian huskies and chow chows, and their even more exotic owners. Who were these people, who could spend a working day in this manner? What a wonderful life it was, I was seeing: people who *lived* near here, in the midst of it all, and could treat their furry buddies to a romp, and stand looking around and thinking, "I live near *here*—the center of it all—wearing a casual wardrobe that drapes very nicely around my large pectoral muscles and/or beautiful breasts. Oh, how I laugh and laugh at that sap at the fence who stares in at me so, like a Victorian child at a toy store window at Christmas, with coal rubbed onto his cheeks, and bad teeth."

One man in particular stood out, a tall handsome athletic guy with a couple of German Shepherds, who looked up at him with a mix of wonder and awe that was almost religious. He was on his phone. Then he looked at his dogs a certain way, and they both—I kid you not—*lay down on the ground and awaited further instructions.*

I watched this, mouth agape, as the seconds ticked into minutes. The dogs watched their master. Their master screamed at someone on the phone, then switched over to another caller, with whom he was equally firm. I couldn't hear what he said, but it sounded very masculine.

On the bench behind him, for humans, sat a long Scandinavian type with tanned legs, a pressed summery yellow short-sleeved shirt, a cute little nose, and tresses of blond hair tied back in a casual ponytail. She smiled at me and stood up.

I could not believe this—she was walking over to me—I was actually thinking how I would tell her I was married . . . when, of course, she slid one of her buttery arms around the tall man's back and he shrugged her off, indicating the phone.

Still, the dogs waited.

The woman bent down to pet the dogs, and the man—he'd finished his call—said something to her and she stood. They kissed. The dogs watched. He gave her (the woman, that is) another command and she retrieved an expensive leather document case that was no doubt his, and very heavy, and slung it over her shoulder. Then the man nodded to his dogs, and they jumped up, following this impossibly good-looking couple as they went for the exit, right next to where I was standing.

The woman opened the gate.

The man—who was two or three inches taller than me, but not much younger—looked down at my reddened eyes and said, "Are you okay?"

He had a British accent, a slight tan.

"How do you do it?" I asked him.

"I'm sorry?"

"What's your secret?" I nodded at the dogs, but also the woman, who was closing the gate behind them. I don't usually respond to strangers, but my review had made me desperate.

"It's simple," he said. "I'm a bastard." He pronounced this, *bahhh-stahd.*

I watched them walk away, this foursome in a dream. The Universe was most definitely telling me something, loud and static-free.

It was saying, "Fuck you."

Envy is power, and my envy of that guy and his life gave me the power to make a start as an Asshole. You'll find that it's harder than it looks. But if Richard Hatch could do it on the first season of *Survivor,* and he made even me look good naked, then I could do it. Or not. I went home feeling overwhelmed, and Gloria proceeded to stoke me right into the game.

She was working part-time at her cooking school, but tonight she was off, watching *Project Runway* reruns on Bravo. When I got back with Hola she asked me how my review had gone.

"Okay," I lied.

I settled on the sofa next to the cat, who never seemed to notice me unless she had something insulting to say.

But Gloria was too smart for my own good. She put the TV on mute. This was something I did all the time—in fact, I greatly preferred all my TV shows with no sound, so I could imagine they were better than they were—but not Gloria. She never muted.

"What happened?" she asked.

On the TV, Heidi Klum was miming her harsh Germanic verdicts to the terrified designers.

"Well," I began, and told Gloria everything. Except the part about the dog park; that was a private man-moment.

My story didn't get the response I expected. Sure, she looked disappointed. But it wasn't like I'd been leaping from triumph to triumph since I'd met her. We had acted in this scene before.

What she said was: "So you're still in the running."

"For what?"

"The promotion. Your boss said they hadn't decided yet."

"Yes, but—"

"But nothing," she interrupted. "You could still get it."

"That's true," I admitted.

"So what if you get this promotion?"

"I dunno," I shrugged. "I'd probably get a window. I'd work more. A bonus."

Gloria sat up straight, which wasn't easy on the chair-and-a-half lounger. *"Bonus?!"*

"In July—end of the fiscal year," I said.

"Okay, so hold on. There's the promotion. How much is that?"

"Just one level—to—"

"No—I don't mean the level, *how much more money?*"

"Oh." I thought. "Not much. Maybe ten or fifteen thousand."

"You can push for more, though?"

"I guess."

"What's the highest?"

"I don't really—"

"Work with me, Marty," she said, swinging her legs off the chair-and-a-half and planting her feet firmly on the sisal rug, facing me. "What's the upper limit—if you yell and scream—I'll coach you on that."

"Maybe twenty thousand," I said.

"Which is how much a month? Less than two? Five hundred a week?"

"Before tax," I pointed out.

"What's the bonus?" she asked, coming over to the sofa and sitting on my right side. The cat jumped off and retreated under the sofa, where things were less intense.

"I don't know."

"Guess. More or less than twenty?"

"It depends. It's twenty per cent usually, but it can go to thirty-five." I thought of Lucifer, the project I was trying to get off the ground. "More if I get this big project sold."

"Oh my God," giggled Gloria, "that's—it's twenty for the raise and thirty-five per cent—"

"At most—"

"How much is that, total? The raise and the bonus?"

I did the math, and said, "Maybe seventy thousand before tax."

"Jesus, how much a month?"

"Six or so—"

"After tax?"

"Maybe a thousand a week."

"Cash in hand? For me to like *spend*?"

"I suppose. But Gloria—"

She was jumping up and down so much and giggling I thought she was going to have a spontaneous clitoral explosion. Maybe she did.

"This is so great." She hugged me. "I can take riding lessons in Van Cortlandt Park like I want to."

"I don't think—"

"Or maybe get a horse—"

"I didn't know—"

"—and I wouldn't have to work as much at the school—"

"You hardly work at—"

"—we could take a great vacation. We could go to Portugal! It's like a dream come true!"

I hated to travel. I said, "I didn't know you wanted to—why would we go to Portugal?"

She broke the bionic bear hug long enough to look at me like I was the stupidest person in Washington Heights. " 'Cause that's where they have the Oliveira Nuño School of Dressage!"

"Dressage?" I was wondering when, exactly, Gloria had become so interested in stallions.

"You really could be a winner, Marty. I can't believe it!"

"Thanks a lot."

"That would be nice, huh?" She was kissing me now, up and down my neck.

"Yuh."

My wife at this point was rather physically energized, running her hands over my back and kissing my chest and collarbone.

"You're gonna get that promotion," she insisted, pulling me up from the couch and leading me by the hand into the pink bedroom.

Let's just say neither of us got much sleep that night. Which was a happy ending to a painful day. But I couldn't help wondering, as I lay there listening to the elevator doors banging through the wall, what would happen if she wasn't right.

STEP ONE

Keep Your Eye on the [Ass]Hole, Not the Donut

"By my foes, sir, I profit in the knowledge of myself."

—William Shakespeare,
Twelfth Night

Having decided to make a start, it's time to focus on where you want to go. There are flyboys out there, men who have polished prickhood to a glossy sheen. And there's a name for such people: co-workers. Also: role models. Go find them. These masters of disaster can be found in almost every neighborhood, office, SUV, reality TV cooking show, and *roman à clef*. Look around. Whether it's your boss, your brother, or the guy who's sleeping with your spouse, these people have what you want. Watch them and learn.

If you open your eyes, you will see Assholes everywhere. I guarantee this in writing. It doesn't even matter where you are, although I understand many of them live in the South. My wife Gloria and I ran into an outstanding example at our car rental place, and he unwittingly guided me to this First Step.

We were standing in line on a Friday afternoon. Let's say there were eight or ten of us at a small car rental facility on the Upper West Side—a long line, for that location. There were three agents behind the counter doing what I assume they were paid to do since they did it every time I was there: stare at their screen, poke at their keyboard, say, "You gotta call the 800 number!," disappear for an hour, make two personal calls, then say, "The system's down." And God help you if you were going to try to redeem frequent-renter points for your car. To do that you had to spend the night on the little couch by the water fountain.

Tension was high. Then someone arrived who took the game to another level.

He was a short man with an unruly, curly mop and glasses he obviously needed, holding a green carry-on bag and a tiny folded umbrella. His American Express Platinum Card was already out as he crashed the front of the line.

"I'm running late, I've gotta emergency!" he growled. "President's Circle member—name's Scheuer."

One of the counter ladies—the one who had spent the last six hours looking for the "Esc" key on her keyboard, and then another two aiming for it with her twelve-inch nail—said, "How you spell that?"

"S-C-H-E-U-E-R."

"Slow down," she requested.

Now, this was New York City. We know what to do with line crashers. Some are given a suspended sentence of immediate banishment from the building, but most are stripped naked and insulted to death. At least, in our minds.

"There's a line," said the woman who was at the front of it.

"Yeah," added someone else.

"I'm running late," said Mr. Scheuer.

"We've been waiting."

"Yeah," whined the guy behind her, "we were here first."

The counter lady asked Mr. Scheuer if a midsize vehicle would be all right.

The short answer was: no. "You get this wrong every time," he sneered. "I can't believe this. I need a full-size—how can you fuck that up all the time?"

"It's not me, sir."

"I don't care," he said. Then a thought occurred to him. "I need a free upgrade—you know how much I spend here. Look that up. You got any Jaguars in?"

"No, sir, we sure don't."

"Don't help him," whined some pathetic guy at the back of the line, "he cut in front." Oh, yeah, that guy was me.

"We have an Escalade," said the counter lady, whistling in admiration. "Only four hundred miles. Practically brand new."

"Sounds okay to me," said Mr. Scheuer. "Throw in a NeverLost with that."

"Already on board, sir."

After he had driven off in his magnificent machine, my wife and I had a couple hours left in the line to ponder what we'd just seen. Our reactions were different. Mine was that it was unfair and poopy and I would get revenge by taking my two hundred dollars of annual business to another rental company, and that would show them. I was livid, although you would never have been able to tell from anything I did.

On the other hand, Gloria started a girl-to-girl round-robin with some people in the line about what a dick that guy was, which somehow morphed into a free mini-seminar on folding omelettes.

I wasn't even listening. In a dark part of my soul, I admired that guy.

He had something I wanted so badly I could smell it. And he reminded me of somebody. It took me a moment to connect the dots, but when I did I realized there was a cesspool of Asshole wisdom right in front of my nose: the Nemesis.

So your first order of business is to find a good role model. If you live and work in America, this won't be hard. It's important to observe the schmuck closely for a period of weeks. It's even more important that you do not let him know what you're doing, for obvious reasons.

I began my field work one night as I was leaving the office. Carrying my travel tote filled with important direct marketing papers, I stopped by the Nemesis's office. He was typing furiously with two fingers and a thumb on his huge Mac computer.

"Hey," I said, buddy to buddy.

He didn't look at me and kept typing.

"Working late, huh?" I asked.

"It's only eight."

"Oh—you're right. Thought it was much, much later."

I stood there for a long time until he finally chose to stop pounding on his innocent keypad and notice me for real. "What's up?"

"How're the projects going?"

"Okay," he said.

"Working on any good pitches?"

"Could be."

"Need any help—?"

"I'll let you know."

He started scrutinizing e-mail on his outsized flat screen. I noticed that his neck was almost bigger around than his head. That must have taken a lot of the kind of weightlifting I didn't even know existed. Did people lift weights with their head? Also, his hands were enormous, and we all know what that means.

On the walls in his office he had an art poster of—I'm not making this up—a credit card, and a framed photograph of an ATM. His desk had a little bobblehead of a St. Louis baseball player, a Rubik's Cube keychain, four staplers, a black Swiss Army jackknife, a scary-looking silver letter-opener, and an unspent round of automatic ammunition.

"Cool," I said. "Lunch next week?"

He looked at me like I'd just taken a dump on his rug.

Just to make sure, I looked down.

Over the course of a week or two, make a careful case study of your role model. Be thorough but quick; he's always moving. Think of it like those documentaries on *Animal Planet* that profile a struggling species and then say it will die out in a few weeks due to an oil spill. The only difference is you are the struggling species, and the role model is the oil spill.

Now I must confess up front that in the course of my time observing the Nemesis in action, I did not see or hear explicit evidence of a number of behaviors you might have expected. For instance, he never actually pummeled a colleague in my presence, at least not physically. He never called a woman a "skanky ho"—although he called many men that. And despite his reputation for having a mercurial temper, I did not see him pistol-whip or machine-gun another VP, at least in the office.

Those are the things he didn't do.

What he gave me were priceless lessons in the ways in which an A-plus Asshole can operate in the corridors of corporate America through a combination of high volume, wild egomania, and a breathtaking lack of social skills. His techniques can usefully be divided into major themes—what we might call The Asshole's Six Secrets of Workplace Effectiveness.

They are, in order of importance:

Number 1. Show No Interest in Others
At first glance, this one may look easy. Most of us are self-centered in the extreme, and it should be no big deal to kick it up a notch or two in order to gain maximum benefit from our hobby. However, the fact is that where true selfishness is concerned, the Nemesis makes us look like Saint Francis.

The Asshole is self-seeking and proud of it; this is America, whose motto was recently changed to "Land of the Me." If there's one more cookie left on the plate, you know who's taking it. If it means standing up for more than ten seconds he's not giving you his seat on the bus. The trouble with the rest of us wannabes is we don't follow through. We fail to take this First Secret literally and show NO—that is, zip, nada, empty circle—interest in others.

We had a regular parade of job candidates coming through our doors to replace the people who had seen the light and left, and we interviewed them in teams. That is, four or five of us at various levels would meet with these people for a half hour, one after another, and grill them on their backgrounds and present a "case," or marketing thought experiment, so they could show us how they'd tackle it. Then after each victim had left we'd meet in the boss's office to debrief and come to a decision.

The Nemesis and I were often on the same interviewing

team, meeting the same candidates and attending the same debriefings. And because my division was about three thousand people stuffed into an office space built for fifty, the interviews usually had to be held in semipublic places like conference rooms—even, one time, on a window ledge next to the copy machine. Thus it was very easy for me to "happen" to overhear the Nemesis "interviewing" a candidate.

His encounters with the candidates were very different from mine. Most of the airtime was eaten up by the Nemesis, in effect, interviewing himself.

"So, walk me through your résumé," he'd start.

"Well, I graduated NYU in—"

"I applied there," he interrupted, "got in. Stern's a good school but you know it's the brand name that really counts. Don't you think? That's why I went to Bowdoin."

"I had a good experience," they'd continue, "particularly in corporate fin—"

"Amazing what's happening east of that neighborhood," he said, stretching wide his arms and yawning, meanwhile unwrapping a bagel he'd forgotten he'd brought with him for breakfast. "I shoulda bought down there five years ago—you know, I've got a building out in Phoenix, I gut rehabbed it. There's a lot of red tape when you renovate. Still it's the best long-term investment—even short-term. Real estate. So where do you live, Steve?"

"Jacob. I live in—"

"They didn't toast this! Man, oh man—they always forget the fucking toasting. How hard is it to do a simple thing like that? I'm gonna have to get another guy fired."

By this point, the candidate was usually staring at the

Nemesis wondering whether maybe he should go back to massage school.

"So what can I tell you about this place?" asked the Nemesis.

"Well, I—"

"You mind if I eat? I went jogging this morning and let me tell you, it's been a while. I'm gonna hit the marathon next year—did that before. I coulda placed higher but there were all those freakin' fat people in my way. They should have a weight limit, at least on the bridges, right? So what job are you up for again?"

And so on. It's amazing he came to any conclusions about any of them. Or not amazing, because he always had the same reaction.

"I didn't like her," he'd say.

"Can you be more specific?" Dale, the HR guy, would ask during the debrief.

"Not sharp enough. Too stupid."

"You say that about all of them."

"That's 'cause the people you're bringing in here are horse shit. Pardon my Uzbeki."

Yet another of his irritating habits: He invented this expression, "Pardon my Uzbeki."

I was known as an "easy interview," respectful and quiet, probing gently into areas where they'd excelled, not too hung up on a "right answer" to the case. They could leave the interview not knowing a single thing about me beyond my name.

And I liked them all. The Nemesis and I always negated one another. We didn't help decide a single hire.

Extreme self-centeredness serves to make others feel small and insecure. You can then jump into the power vacuum, and start taking names.

Number 2. Speak Loudly, Interrupt Often

The Nemesis liked to interrupt early and often. Think about what it does: shuts people down. It's pure and simple dominance in the human animal kingdom. I'm talking—you talk *over* me. I stop. You control the frame.

Outside skilled eye contact, interrupting may be the single biggest pellet in the Asshole's shotgun. Much more important than what you say is *when* you say it.

Consistency is also important—as in, acting like a broken record. Changing your mind, listening to reason, these are the fatal weaknesses of the Castrated Beta Male (CBM).

One time we had a guest speaker come in to talk to us about women small business owners as consumers. She was highly prepared, with a slick slide show, young but articulate and dressed in dark blue slightly above the occasion, and her opinions were more than usually grounded in data.

"What we see," she said, "is women are very responsive to messages with seasonal language. Talking about Renewal and the Spring and even what seems like old-fashioned stuff—oh, Harvest-time and Back-to-School—all that really resonates with this audience. We think that's because women are—well, they're more seasonal or cyclical biologically if you know what I—"

"I don't know about that," interrupted the Nemesis, chomping on some Cool Ranch Doritos from a little bag in his lap and almost yelling. "You're talkin' about cycles and stuff but actually running a business is a—"

"Can we save the questions till after," she said.

"—It isn't a question, it's an answer."

Nervous laughter.

"Let me tell you something about women," he went on. "I

know women. And this seasonal stuff is total shit. Pardon my Uzbeki. Women are always in a bad mood and it doesn't even matter what part of the year we're in. And they're really messy. Let me tell you, my girlfriend . . ."

We were treated to an oration on the Nemesis's knowledge of women, which seemed to consist mostly of things he'd picked up in the group showers back at Delta Gamma house. This guy knew women like I knew dog training.

What surprised me more was that he was not married. Mostly because he regularly rhapsodized about the great wit and wisdom of "my incredible wife, Mary."

But only when clients were in the room.

The magic of interruption is that it puts others on the defensive, forcing them to react. You control the conversation. The person you interrupt then gets all flustered and wheezy, as our speaker did at that moment.

Number 3. Claim Every Idea You've Ever Heard as Your Own
I highly recommend this technique. It seems like it wouldn't work, but that's precisely why it does. Most people are afraid to make bold statements in case they're caught in a lie, forgetting that nobody has the time or inclination to fact-check anything. Plus, people are ignorant. Say confidently that you're a state senator and nine out of ten people will believe you, because they have no idea who the state senators are, or even what one is.

My observations of the Nemesis suggest that good credit-gathering does require care. But as long as you're not claiming ownership of some idea in front of the actual inventor—or saying something outrageous like you created the question mark—you're okay.

My week of anthropology included an office "team building"

event, a scavenger hunt around mid-Manhattan and a party at a bar in South Harlem. The Nemesis helped design the hunt and competed, and his team won. Big surprise. I went up to him at the after-party to pick his brain. He was guzzling a green beverage.

"This drink is weak," he said. "*Caipirinha*. You know I was a bartender in college—I came up with the mint leaves idea. It really caught on."

"You invented the *caipirinha*?" I asked.

He smiled. "So how's the new card project going?"

"Okay—"

"I mentioned to Liz"—she was my client for the project he referred to—"it would be cool to hold an ideation workshop. I'm glad she went with it."

"I thought she—"

"You know I've been telling them for a while now they need to streamline their merchant data clusters, and I think they're gonna do it. We're on the verge of a half-million-dollar sell-in with them."

"Who? What?"

"You like this bar? I picked it out. Thought it would be a cool place for a work thing, you know?"

He was relentless, and it had a cumulative effect. Some happiness gurus say the key to equanimity is to practice gratitude throughout the day for every little thing—"I'm grateful for warm water, I'm grateful for my pillow," et cetera—and, in aggregate, you end up more joyful. The same principle was at work here: The Nemesis took credit throughout the day for every little thing, and he ended up impressing even the most cynical listener as an ass . . . but an important, influential ass.

Number 4. Never, Ever Admit to a Mistake

The Nemesis never once admitted to being wrong, mistaken, misguided, or even vaguely askew.

His brand of infallibility was most obvious during our regular VP postmortems, when we gathered as a management team to go over those frequent occasions when we'd failed to land a project or account, or we'd somehow not delivered as expected. These were occasions for frank humility and pledges to do better.

Unless, of course, you were the Nemesis.

One time we VPs were assembled in the corner conference room looking down on Eighth Avenue and the blinds were pulled. We were talking about a failed pitch for a project to use data about what people buy in one type of store (say, Home Depot) to predict what they might buy in another type of store (say, The Gap). Kind of like retail cross-addiction psychoanalysis.

The Nemesis had led the team that lost to a very smart group from Digitas—not that you'd know it from what he said.

"What was the feedback?" asked our boss, running her fingers through her hair.

"She was incredibly impressed and, I think, totally into working with us next go-round," said the Nemesis.

"Anything else?"

"Hmmm . . . just that it went great."

"So why did we lose the pitch?"

The Nemesis started squeezing the impressive bicep bulging under his no-iron shirt. He did this when he was angry. "Maybe they knew somebody. I think one of their guys may have gone to school with her sister—or something."

"She said that to you?"

"Not exactly. But you know." He winked at the boss, or maybe something was stuck in his eye.

"So," pressed the boss, "there wasn't anything about the content? Suggestions for improvement? She liked our approach?"

"She didn't like it," said the Nemesis, "she *loved* it. Those are words she used. I'd say the meeting went as great as it could have for us."

"But still we lost. Amazing."

"Maybe we were too good," I said, in what I hoped was a highly ironic tone of voice. "Maybe they were intimidated by our great intelligence."

Instead of rising to my bait, the Nemesis shrugged and took a bite from his extra-garlic bagel.

"You could be right," he said.

This Secret also builds beautifully on human beings' natural insecurity and ignorance. The simple truth is nobody knows anything, and by confidently pretending you're better than human you'll fool more people than you won't. You'll be lying, of course, but an Asshole finds truth optional.

Number 5. Criticize in Public, Praise in Private

We had an all-staff meeting shortly after the postmortem, and the Nemesis displayed a trait that—more than any other except, perhaps, his love of the extra-garlic bagel—made me idolize him as a pharmaceutical-grade Asshole.

Our department of fifty-odd young people was gathered around a large conference table, going over odds and ends. After we'd introduced the new additions to the team and done announcements ("The date for the move to the nineteenth floor is finalized," "SAS training is mandatory for managers," et cetera), the boss went over new business and pitches that we'd lost. The Nemesis was asked, per custom, to share a few words on his cross-store promotion debacle.

"It went great," he said, echoing what he'd told the VPs, "and the team worked hard. But we didn't win it—and that doesn't make me happy. Let's learn from this."

Here, he sat up straighter and made eye contact around the table, person by person. He stopped on Todd, the guy I'd seen him berating before my review.

"Now Todd needs to check his work more carefully. Quality control—that's what we need. You're new here but that's no excuse. Some of the numbers in Todd's item list didn't add up, and I didn't get a chance to look it over. And Sarah's slides were too busy on the screen." He shifted his focus to Sarah. "It's okay for reading, but it got in the way when it's projected. Work at it."

There was an exception to the Nemesis's policy of blaming everything on others. That was when a project went well. Then, of course, he didn't mention a single other name. His triumphs were solo flights.

Later that afternoon, I happened to walk past his office when he had Todd the Loser in with him.

"I really appreciate all you're doing," I heard him say to Todd, sounding sincere. "You're helping me out."

"But in that meeting you said—"

"We're not all detail people, right?"

He noticed me lingering, so I moved on, realizing I'd found the secret to the Nemesis's ability to keep his teams working late into the night, on weekends, and once (as rumor had it) during a close relative's actual funeral service.

Two words: *mind games.*

Subtle psychological torture works powerfully in keeping

your underlings in a perpetual state of self-doubt and fear. Total confusion softens them into the right frame of mind to be victimized.

Number 6. Know What You Want

I have to give the Nemesis credit for something: He knew how to *focus.*

Like an elite athlete who trains for years to get to a point where not a single motion is wasted, he had calibrated his mind and body to filter out everything that didn't directly contribute to his goal.

Or, rather, goals. It's obvious he wanted both money *and* power.

He wouldn't waste time with you if you could not help him on his way. And if you could, he'd give you so much attention you might consider taking out a restraining order or at least pretending you were on the phone every time you saw him coming.

The Nemesis is like the CEO who's paid $200 million in a bad year, a jackpot hundreds of thousands of people—even dozens of his own ex-wives—know he does not deserve. Yet he gets the money. Why? Because he's charmed or blackmailed about *five people*—i.e., the Compensation Committee of the Board of Directors. In the entire world, *vis-à-vis* his payday, those are the people who count, and they are the *only* ones.

So put yourself in any workplace situation. Think about your goal. What is it? Focus on what it takes to get there. All the rest is donkey shit. Pardon my Uzbeki.

Sometimes others can help us when our sight grows dim. As when Gloria called me at my desk, as she did so often, and asked: "How's our bonus coming along, peanut?"

• • •

My preliminary studies of the genus *Nemesis* were almost complete. I'd observed him in his habitat and taken extensive mental notes on his behaviors and habits. One time I even followed him into the men's room, but the less said about that incident the better. All that was left was for me to take him into neutral territory—somewhere outside the office, beyond its lusts, resentments, and kleptomaniacal vending machines.

You may recall I invited the Nemesis out to lunch a few weeks earlier during a moment of insanity, and now I was forced to make good on my threat. Although about as much fun for me as pulling hair out of my nose with tweezers (which I do, by the way), it was a golden opportunity to see some of my role model's Secrets up close.

We went to the Gold Lion on 45th Street and walked down the steps to the subterranean entrance. Cesar Millan, the Dog Whisperer, says that in order to establish dominance over your canine you should always walk through every door *in front* of the dog; also, while en route you need to make sure your knees are *in front* of the dog's nose.

The Nemesis walked most of the way from the office to the Gold Lion about a hundred yards in front of me. Not only did he go through the restaurant's door first, but he was already working on my appetizer by the time I arrived.

I had actually tried—as an experiment—to get ahead of him on the sidewalk. When I moved up, he walked faster and faster, until both of us were sprinting down the street without acknowledging what was going on.

Maybe he didn't know what he was doing. Maybe it was second nature.

After we'd ordered, I interrupted a speech he was making on the declining brand value of Lindsey Lohan with a question: "Can I ask you something?"

"In a second—" (Secret #6)

After many seconds, during which he outlined his inane suggestions to revitalize Lindsey's image, I tried again: "So I wanted to ask you—"

Louder: "Hold on—so then I—" (Secret #2)

ME: (much later) "I like your style, man. Where did you learn how to manage people so incredibly well?" (Applying Secret #5)

HIM: "Are you fucking with me?"

ME: "No, really. I want to be more like you. How do you get people to do what you want? Do you give them a lot of encouragement?"

HIM: (howling with laughter) "Ha ha ha! Ha!! That's a good one! Now I know you're fucking with me! Pardon my Uzbeki."

ME: "But seriously. Don't you worry about hurting their feelings?"

HIM: "Feelings? What are those?" (Secret #1)

ME: "Things that make us laugh and cry—"

HIM: "You know what hurts my feelings, Marty? And promise me this goes no farther than this table. Can I have that dumpling? What makes me sad—when a chick doesn't understand a 'one-night stand' means *just one night*."

ME: "Ah."

HIM: "Anyway, I'll tell you something my dad told me when I was a kid, like five years ago. We were lifting

weights in the basement and between sets he said
to me: '[Nemesis], son, always remember your
employees don't have hopes and dreams. They have
billable hours.' (Misting up) I'll always remember
that." (Secret #1)

ME: "What did your dad do?"

HIM: "He drove a cab. So, anyway, what did you want
to talk about?"

At this point, I really had no idea.

So I asked him if he thought he'd get promoted this round.
Suddenly, he remembered a place he had to be like ten minutes
ago. The last thing he said to me before he grabbed what was
left of my lunch was, "Update your résumé, ha ha."

Though he was always eating he was not an overweight person. All those wild mood swings no doubt strained his system.
And the sessions punishing the weight stacks in the gym pulled
all the blood away from his brain and deposited it directly into
his sense of entitlement.

Wending my lone way back down 45th Street past Eighth to
my office, I pondered what I had learned. First, the Nemesis
was paranoid. Super-paranoid. Second, he saw the world as full
of incompetent people who were continually leaving a bad taste
in his mouth like secondhand smoke.

That's probably why he forgot to leave me any money for the
check.

Not long after that lunch, I turned on the TV and happened to
stumble across an even better Asshole role model than the
Nemesis.

My new hero arrived on TNT in the form of a rebroadcast of Brian De Palma's 1983 film *Scarface,* starring Al Pacino and Michelle Pfeiffer and written by Oliver Stone. I'd thought of *Scarface* before as a real touchstone of the Asshole worldview, and I'd always appreciated its large firearms, but the fact that it was being shown that very night seemed inspired by God.

As you know, *Scarface* is the touching story of a Cuban thug named Tony Montana, played by Pacino, who lands in Miami in 1980 and gets into the cocaine trade, rising through a combination of his own ruthlessness and a total disregard for, well, for everything to a position approaching world domination.

A lot of people I know think Tony Montana is stupid. But he has a simple philosophy of life, one that centers around a single part of his anatomy:

- "All I have in this world are *balls*—and my word!" says Tony.
- "I need a guy with steel in his *balls*, Tony. A guy like you," says his boss.
- And most disturbingly, in Tony's words: "The only thing in this world that gives orders is *balls!*"

I studied Tony's body language. No smile, of course, but I was surprised to see his mouth is usually closed. His chin is out—what I would come to learn was basic alpha male symbology. Not only is his eye contact constant, but also he doesn't blink. Watch him. It's weird. Pacino's eyeballs must have felt like sandpaper by the second day of filming.

The gaze is continuous, as I've said, but only when he's *talking,* not when he's listening, with one exception. He pays attention at all times when someone is pointing a gun at him.

Aggressiveness isn't an occasional thing, either—he signals it with a pimp-like roll, leading with his prick like it's a pet, and a thrust-out chest. "Me," he says, "I always tell the truth. Even when I lie." Whatever that means.

At one point Tony's best friend pays his buddy the highest compliment one person can pay to another: "You're an asshole, man!"

Not that I would advise you to emulate Tony Montana completely—he keeps a live tiger in his backyard, after all, and as his mother points out he tends to "destroy everything." But after Tony swan dives off a balcony into a pool of his own blood and the closing credits roll, I defy you not to feel an upswell of elation . . . you have found your role model. The perfect Asshole.

In fact—now that I thought about it—isn't the Asshole actually a new kind of man? The next stage in the evolution of the American male? Consider this. My father's generation was, he frequently tells me, quite a bit more polite than mine; and kids today seemed totally debased to me. Compare Cary Grant to Johnny Knoxville. Nice guys used to run things, sometimes; now they don't even get the key to the men's room.

Apparently there was a time in American history when people used to share things, like needles. There were whole decades when otherwise rational men and women wasted money on terrible investments, like their church. Entire months when actual human beings said things like "make love, not war," and "give peace a chance" without peeing in their pants laughing. Luckily, we'd moved on.

Rather than devolving into a more primitive state, maybe I was nudging the race toward some incredible future condition.

Take a look at where you are, and where you could be going:

The ASS-cent of Man

	BETA MALE	ALPHA MALE	ASSHOLE
Car Brand	Toyota	Porsche	Hummer
Cable Channel	CNN	CNBC	Fox News
Secret Vice	Al Gore	Red Bull	Polygamy
Primate	Chimp	Gorilla	King Kong
Religion	Agnosticism	Atheism	Jism
Pet	Cat	Dog	Co-worker
Investment	Index funds	Stocks	Fraud
Video Game	The Sims	Grand Theft Auto	Offshore gambling
Charity	PETA	Ex-wife	NASCAR
Prescription	Prozac	Lipitor	Nitroglycerin
Loves	You	Work	n/a
Hates	Lint	Interruptions	You

STEP TWO

Get a Life (Coach)

"Take three months to prepare your machines."

—Sun Tzu,
The Art of War

You don't have a clue what you're doing or you wouldn't be reading this sentence. So why would you rely on yourself to mastermind the most important transformation of your life—from zero to hero, twitchy to bitchy, gawky to cocky? Find qualified professionals to help you mobilize your mission. These men and women are there to provide practical knowledge and common-sense advice that Assholes already know but you do not.

Locating the correct coach is not easy. But considering your pathetic starting point, almost anyone can help you. I mean this literally: Go out into the street, tap someone at random, and chances are they've forgotten more about dickdom than you ever knew. Whoever you end up enlisting, just take their best, ignore the rest, and fire them. Remember: If they make you uncomfortable, you're going in the right direction. Pain is prelude.

The Nemesis had set the bar dauntingly high for me. But he had a lifetime's headstart and a steroid addiction to help him. I wasn't sure where to turn, so I did what I always do when I'm confused: took a class. It was a seminar held in midtown called "How to Be a Bitch."

That's right—Bitch, not Asshole. It turns out that all of the seminars, classes, and self-help groups that have formed around making people less nice have one thing in common: *They're for women.*

I didn't understand this at all. In my experience, women are on average a lot less nice than the men I've known. And the worst of them wind up in Manhattan, where they assemble in covens in the dead of night to plan their takeover, of not only the men on the island, but the entire world order. Or so I imagined. Meanwhile, most of the men I've known are full of self-doubt and fear and don't just *think* they'd be making a lot more money if they were more the big dick—they *know* it.

So I ended up at this Bitch workshop, and when I got there—big surprise—I was the only man. There were thirty or so plain-looking middle-aged women, me, and a couple young women from other countries sitting up front, who were probably lost. I got some double takes, but these ladies were much too nice to say anything about my gender issue.

The teacher was a short-haired Asian woman named Tina.

She said: "Being nice is just a bad habit—and habits can be changed. It's about being *dishonest,* and it's about having *no passion.* That's it. You know what the word 'nice' meant in Middle English? It meant 'foolish.'

"It's a spiritual problem," she continued. "A denial of what's real. What we're doing when we're acting nice is denying our right to exist. This isn't about the rational mind. That just wants the status quo. It's about the soul—the higher self that wants to be free to be itself."

Before we could finish writing this pearl into our notebooks, Tina heaped another problem onto us. She told us we were in fact servants "with six billion masters."

"Why six billion?" she asked. "Because that's the number of people in the world. That's who we're looking to for approval. Nice people are weird," she chanted, preaching to the choir. "We're like control freaks in the middle of a hurricane. Trying to manipulate things that cannot be manipulated."

She asked us, "What are nice people trying to control? It's their own *fear*. But like the *Tao* says—or the *I Ching*, I forget— you can't lose something if it's really yours. Think about it. You *can't* lose it, if it's yours."

I started wondering how that rule applied to things like car keys, and I guess my mind wandered because I suddenly realized the room had become very quiet, and the entire class was staring at me. Tina had asked me something and was waiting for an answer.

"I'm sorry," I said. "What'd you say?"

"Don't apologize," she told me. "I asked you what your *passion* is."

There are a number of questions nobody should have to answer on the spot. What is your I.Q.? Do you think I'm gaining weight? Why don't you have children? What's your passion?

"Well . . . I . . . I . . ."

"That's my point," said Tina. "We're passionless people. Nice people have robbed themselves of *life*."

While I am delighted to help any teacher prove a point, it

seemed unfair what she'd done to me. I had passion, plenty of passion. I passionately hated the Nemesis, for one thing. I passionately hated my current apartment. I passionately . . . maybe that was it, but it was a great start.

"Decide what you want and pursue it with *vitality*," she said, looking right at me.

Nice was slavery, she said.

Nice was death.

Nice was not nice.

I was still upset about that passion crack, so I withdrew into myself—then realized I was proving just how far I was from my own goal. I still wasn't exactly sure what an Asshole was, but I was pretty sure he wouldn't give a shit if some skinny hippie called him passionless. I was pretty sure he'd think: *Smoke my pole!*

"How are you feeling now?" she asked me. Me, again. She had a fetish.

"Fine," I said.

"No, you're not. You're upset with what I just said earlier. You've been stewing on it. Am I right?"

I said nothing.

"Tell me one thing. You're uncomfortable right now, right?"

"I don't—"

"Just answer me that."

I stared at her blankly. "What's the question again?"

One of the young women in the front row laughed.

"You're uncomfortable? Yes or no."

"I am now," I admitted.

"Good. Stay with it. See—" said Tina, getting off her stool for the first time and standing slightly lopsided, as though one of her legs was a prosthesis she got on sale—"nice people have another thing in common. We're *uncomfortable being uncomfortable.*"

She let that sink in. I was uncomfortable. Was I uncomfortable being uncomfortable? That thought made me uncomfortable. So I was going through at least two, and maybe three, existential layers of discomfort when Tina finally broke the silence by flinging a felt-tip pen at me.

Of course she claimed it was an accident. She didn't apologize—that would have been passionless. And I didn't apologize when I got up and walked out of the room.

When I got home, I asked Gloria if she thought I had vitality. It was kind of hard to talk to her since she was doing her kickboxing exercises while watching Rachael Ray on the Food Network.

"Like how do you mean?" she asked, before roundhousing our bamboo plant and screaming, *"Geee!"*

I sat down on the sofa and opened a cool Dr. Pepper and a package of Ring Dings. "Like in life," I said, "do you feel like you need a passion? Or is that more optional?"

"Geee-yup! Hoo-ay-yow!"

"Come again?"

"It's important," she panted. "Everybody knows that. And right now we're passionate about your promotion. How's it going?"

The Bitch seminar was not all I had hoped it would be. I'm entirely in favor of woman power, but not for men. So I decided to try some one-on-one training. I needed help, and not the kind of specialized help a mere career advisor or corporate image consultant could give me—no, I decided I needed help with, well, with *everything*. My entire life.

I needed a Life Coach.

The one I hired was a clinically obese older woman named Dr. Strong, who wore a festive head scarf and had a manic laugh and ADHD. Also she was a Luddite. I know this because she spent most of our first hour abusing her portable CD player for not emitting the soothing sounds of surf and gulls.

We sat on plastic folding chairs facing one another. The CD player was in her lap, and also in the air, as she repeatedly picked it up to shake. Behind Dr. Strong, sitting on a high shelf, was one of those small Japanese rock waterfalls you can order in a catalog, but the water wasn't running.

"So you want to be more assertive," she said.

"No, it's more than that," I told her. "I want to be an Asshole."

"You want to be *asshole*?"

"Yup."

"As in, rear end of person?"

"Yup."

"Not just assertive?"

"No—that's not gonna do it. I want to be truly objectionable—like the kind of person people go out of their way to avoid."

"You want to be *avoided*?" She turned the player upside down and hit it.

"No—I just don't want to care anymore. I want people to listen to me—I want to—I just want *to get my way in this fucking city*."

"Uh huh."

"I know this sounds weird," I said, "but I'm so tired of being the nicest guy in the world."

"Why you so nice? Huh?"

Good question. Dr. Strong asked me to close my eyes and form a mental image of my ideal self.

"What you see?" she prodded.

"Myself."

"As you are now?"

"Yes."

"No! Not right! Think what you *want to be* . . . Mister Marty Man-Pants. *Him* is in your mind. Fucking motherfuck," she whispered, banging on the CD player. "So what you see now? *Goddamn this thing!—*"

It's not so easy for a guy like me to imagine what I want to be. I'm so used to framing things in the negative: I only really knew what I wanted *not* to be. Maybe I should try living as Opposite Marty; it had worked for George Costanza.

"You got picture yet?" she asked me.

This is what I described to Dr. Strong:

I wake up and the sun is shining—my windows no longer look out on an airshaft. Light! Glorious sunlight! I am naked, but this is not so frightening as it could be as I am in much better shape. Like a Men's Life *version of myself. I roll over and bump into my wife. We're both so incredibly gorgeous that I can't help but take a moment or two to admire our bodies in the large mirror mounted on the ceiling above us. Gloria's enormously enhanced breasts are a particular treat.*

Our dog, Hola, I notice, is waiting patiently by the side of the bed with a chew toy in her mouth—the quiet kind, which she now prefers. It's clear from her eager expression she lives only to do my bidding and awaits my command. Gloria has a similar look, actually. She asks me if I'd like more sex before breakfast, and I say, "Gotta run. Big meeting."

The crushing disappointment in her face bodes well for tonight.

Our apartment is immaculate, thanks to our obsessive-compulsive maid. She also walks the dog. And is Brazilian. And beautiful. Also single. Her worship of me causes some tension in my marriage, but I'm pretty sure Gloria's on the verge of agreeing to a three-way.

I dress entirely in black silky-smooth fabrics and mirror-shades. On my way out, the doorman not only holds the door wide open for me but actually salutes my retreating figure as I leave the building. A couple guys I pass on the street salute me also, I'm not sure why.

I pass my neighbor, Ramón, who looks terrible, like he hasn't slept in a week and has been living on nothing but Yodels. His dog, Misty, is gnawing on his ankles like a demented gerbil.

I ignore them. At Twin Donut my order is sitting on the counter in a special Plexiglas case designed to keep the corn muffin fresh and the coffee at optimum temperature. The case has a sign: "SENOR MARTY MUFFIN, ONLY—KEEP OUT! THIS MEAN YOU!!"

As I remove my package, the entire staff of Twin Donut is bowing to me from behind the counter, their eyes averted.

I leave without paying. The manager says, "An extra large muffin—new invention!"

I get to work in no time and am greeted with a group hug by all the women who work for me. I head for the corner office, which has my name on it, ignoring the SVPs' compliments hurled at me in the hallways, and turn to scream some orders at the man sitting in the secretary's chair outside my office.

It's the Nemesis. He's wearing an apron, has lost most of his hair, weighs like three hundred pounds, is drooling, and has a little statue of me on top of his computer monitor.

"Get me my fucking schedule," I say, and slam the door behind me.

I return calls of important people and have work meetings with colleagues who generally have a look of fear mixed with awe as I speak. I can't remember most of their names and I don't know if they're any good at their jobs, because I don't listen to a word they say.

When I want to hear a brilliant idea, I just talk.

Later, the Nemesis comes in. It's time for his performance review. I toss away the actual performance review and say, "You're really fucking up, Barry—"

"That's not my na—"

"I've invented something I like to call the 'Back-Track,' since it involves a series of demotions until you're either working in the mailroom or you kill yourself."

"Thank you, sir."

"I'm thinking of rolling it out office-wide."

"You are generous to a fault."

"Don't I know it," I snort.

That night I'm driven to an A-list party somewhere hot I don't know about yet with the biggest reality TV stars and celebrity podcasters. Uma Thurman is there and—

Suddenly, in my fantasy, I notice the cool party has become warmer, and I'm sweating. Uma looks uncomfortable, then she disappears. My designer shirt is soaked through and—

My eyes snapped open. I was alone in the room.

Despite that unsettling beginning, I persisted in my work with Dr. Strong, meeting each Wednesday at lunchtime for two months. In my second session she introduced me to what she called "Secret Weapon." Excited at first by the chance to own such a Weapon, I grew more skeptical in time. I mean, she had a different Secret Weapon every week. It was psychotherapeutic nuclear proliferation.

The most useful was an image I recommend you use in your journey. I'd been complaining that I was still too nice and I wasn't making progress. About the only thing I'd done that seemed like a concrete Asshole step was buy a new ringtone for my phone. Now whenever anyone called me there was Ice-T's voice saying: *"Pick up the phone, player! Big money on the line!"*

It was something, but it wouldn't get me promoted.

The image Dr. Strong planted in my mind was this: Imagine you [that is, I] are yourself, sitting at a business meeting, or walking down the street. Now imagine getting bigger and bigger, until you're the size of a giant. Now turn yourself into a robot, made entirely out of steel. Give yourself laser cannons under your arms and a laser site mounted on your helmet.

When that image is clear in your mind, encase yourself in a plastic bubble made of impenetrable plastic. You can see out of the bubble, but nothing can get through. Dr. Strong called this the "plastic bubble-shield," and I conjured it up in my mind many times each day for months.

It's harder to worry who you're stepping on when you're made of steel and have a head-mounted laser site. When Gloria caught me practicing this—I didn't tell her why—she said I looked like Marty Feldman in *Young Frankenstein*.

Dr. Strong took me through the visualization . . . step by step . . . deeper and deeper into a state of total relaxation. I remember drifting out of the room, walking around Manhattan like a character in an old Japanese horror film. I felt the air get warmer—

Again my eyes snapped open. Dr. Strong was gone. Again. I had fallen asleep, and again she had left me. The rising temperature was due to the fact that the building's air conditioning had been turned off, which offices usually only do when it's late. And all the doors were locked.

Unbelievable.

There was a note, on the chair where Dr. Strong had been. It read: *"See you next time, 'Asshole'—Me."* There was also a cheaply printed color brochure titled MEDITATION & VISUALIZATION FOR GROWTH.

On this she had written with a black Sharpie pen, "TRY ME."

At this stage in our journey, it's important we be able to eliminate the clutter of our current lives, assumptions, parents, pets—everything that distracts us from our goal. We need to focus. One of the best ways to get your mind in shape for what is to come is the following practice:

MEDITATION FOR ASSHOLES

My method can be practiced in the morning, during your commute, at your desk, after tai chi—whenever you want. The purpose is to clear your mind of all nice, helpful, self-defeating thoughts and replace them with mean, selfish, and ass-kicking patterns that will help you get ahead (and get head).

There are four components: Breathing, Visualizing, Affirmations, and Prayer.

Breathing—Sit in a comfortable place. Close your eyes. Try to cleanse your mind of all thoughts and images that are tranquil or soothing. Breathe in, breathe out. Imagine your breath is a liquid, like a river, only full of medical waste and dead sea animals.

Alter breathing so your mouth is closed on the inhale, for a count of two, then it opens on the inhale, as it closes for the subsequent exhale. And the opposite goes for your nostrils. Make sure they are shut tight for the exhales, until the fourth exhale (counting, of course, the in-breaths as one and the out-breaths as one-and-one-half breaths).

At this point, if you've followed my directions, you should be trying to breathe in with both your mouth and your nostrils shut tight. You will then pass out, after seeing a flash of white light that signals your brain synapses shutting down.

See, you really are a people-pleasing *putz!* How hard is it to breathe, for God's sake? You don't need a guidebook for that.

So breathe. Now you're ready for . . .

Visualizing—You need to build an "unsafe space." This is an unsettling, fear-soaked room you can return to again and again as a base for your visualization work. Making this space as upsetting and dark as possible is important. I like to see myself, in my mind's eye, in a very small room strewn with various sharp objects and Polaroids of my ex-girlfriends, especially the ones who dumped me. There is nowhere to sit, screeching speed metal music is playing, alternating with the greatest hits of Michael McDermott.

Affirmations—Affirmations are mean-spirited statements you can incorporate into your meditation practice, and repeat throughout the day.

What follows are a few I've found helpful, but you should also write your own:

- I love myself unconditionally, as long as I'm perfect
- There is nothing I set my mind on I can't accomplish through intimidation
- I constantly feel a nameless dread which inspires me

Prayer—If meditation is our act of listening to ourselves, then prayer is more about talking. Rather than to God, however, we are praying to ourselves—our own Higher Power. I repeat the following regularly at night before I go to sleep:

May my adversaries be agitated, unhappy, and hypoglycemic. May they continually encounter difficulties, self-doubt, and feelings of inadequacy. May these feelings be entirely accurate and impossible to escape, even through the sweet deliverance of sleep, which shall become for them a nightmarescape of shapeless mammals and badly-lit images from Japanese horror films with little kids screaming. And may they never understand why they can't seem to get a good haircut, even at expensive places.

Meditation is like medication—a lot of fun, but not a great substitute for leaving the house. In addition to your spiritual work, you must continue to monitor your Asshole role model for nuggets of nastiness. I continued to learn more from my opponent than from the disappointing coaches I had found so far.

The division I worked for did direct marketing, which is all the advertising you actively loathe, such as junk mail, online banners and pop-up ads, and—horror of horrors—unsolicited phone calls on weekends and during dinner. This, as opposed to the advertising you merely detest, such as car commercials.

Embarrassed by the phone calls, we referred to them only by their acronym, OBTM—Outbound Telemarketing. And junk mail was called DM, for Direct Mail. All Online Advertising was OLA, like my dog, but without the "H," for "Happily-eating-daddy's-shoes-right-now."

On the other hand, our sister divisions did the kind of advertising that was far sexier, such as TV spots and spreads in fashion magazines. Although we had grown rapidly during the dot-com rebound, Direct Marketing still hadn't quite shaken off its reputation as the place where losers, nerds, and the genetically uncool went to die.

There was even a height difference. What the TV and print guys did was called Above-the-Line (ATL). What we did was Below-the-Line (BTL).

Emily and Eleanor had just finished up a project for me that had gone over well. It was about as BTL as it gets: figuring out the best place to put legalistic "fine print" on a corporate website. Glamour was not a big part of our job description. Despite their youth—or maybe because of it—these women were a lot of fun to work with. Emily's strong feelings about everything were balanced out by Eleanor's cool grace, and they were far from lazy.

As a reward, and because I liked their company, I asked them to tag along with me to the client's offices. I sat between the Nemesis and our division's Executive Vice President, a "blond," big-boned, comically outgoing woman fighting sixty. Across the table were some clients and the "brand guys"— vaguely influential executives from the ATL side of our company. From time to time we were forced to work together, so the junk mail and spam didn't conflict with the TV and so on. But ATL's idea of working together generally had them doing a lot of talking, and us doing a lot of nodding.

So the brand guy, in a pink shirt with a yellow tie, was talking in front of a screen projecting images of adorable kittens frolicking on a green lawn, and I was nodding.

". . . and what you need to keep in mind," he said, "is that there literally is no limit to the number of kittens we can put in this spot. There's an innate unconscious affinity that the human female has for baby felines that drives a powerful purchase response—"

"How do we know that?" challenged the Nemesis. He was sitting straight up, glaring at the brand guy, and his hand came down on the table in a chop-chop.

"Well. The research tells us—"

"What research?"

"F-focus groups in fourteen markets. But my point is—"

The Nemesis shook his head and chop-chopped again, raising his voice. "I'd have to say they're wrong," he said.

"What?"

"My gut tells me kittens depress the purchase cycle because they call up nurturing emotionality. Now nurturing is an anti-consumerist impulse—"

"Tell that to P&G—"

"Let me finish—is anti-consumerist in the financial products market. Not consumer goods."

He kept going for a while—but what impressed me, as usual, was that he disagreed. The Nemesis *always* disagreed. Here he was challenging something that was so obviously true it was a total cliché—that is, women like kittens—and saying it was false. Black was white. Nemesis was President. It was so beautifully executed, it all but took my breath away.

At the end of the meeting, the Nemesis literally grabbed the EVP's arm and interposed himself between her and me in the car on the way back downtown. Although the ride was almost forty minutes through dense traffic, I did not exchange a single word with either of them. Demonstrating their superior intelligence, Emily and Eleanor had taken a different cab.

The Nemesis went on and on about how little baby kittens were the Antichrist, psycho-demographically speaking. What an asshole.

To help me understand my new idol better, over the next couple of days I combed through the academic literature on assertiveness and "Machiavellianism." The latter turned out to be a well-established workplace style characterized by "manipulative strategies of social conduct." The prick who used this style liked to treat others, in the words of one expert, "as objects to be controlled to meet his or her self-focused goals."

Exactly! I thought. I read on.

One study of Machiavellian salespeople in the *Journal of Business Ethics* showed they were more successful than nicer peers but got lower ratings from their supervisors. Despite extensive use of "ingratiation and flattery," these jerks had a low desire for acceptance by the group.

Assholism was associated with being younger, later-born, and female (told you). So older, first-born males (like me) tended to be nicer (like me). And there was an interesting study of accountants done in 2006, described in the *International Journal of Management Practice,* that indicated dingleberries had more clients *even though they performed worse.* Being a dickhead made you money in spite of incompetence.

Other studies showed jerkitude in the workplace was associated with being intelligent. Smarter people tended to be less easy-going, perhaps because they understood the consequences of niceness. Which garnered, according to *Personnel Psychology,* fewer promotions than were given more assertive colleagues.

There was also evidence that acting like an Asshole made you feel the world was a fairer place, because you felt free to speak your mind and therefore did not suffer (as I did) in silence. You felt better about life even if you didn't get the promotion.

One particularly disturbing report in the *Journal of Social and Clinical Psychology* showed that Machiavellian types often do not choose to act as they do—that the Machiavellian is "a person who is unconnected to his or her own emotion" and lacks empathy. Many of them may suffer from a condition called "alexithymia," or an inability to know what they and others are feeling. In other words, a sociopath.

Oh, to be that blessed.

And a study comparing the attitudes of Midwestern college students today with those of the 1960's came to the conclusion that—as a society—we are definitely getting more Machiavellian.

Tell me something I don't know.

A few nights later, I was watching Gloria cut up a chicken while I worked on my hair to go out. I'd adopted a moussing regimen that required careful comb work, which I preferred to do away from the mirror so that I didn't have to see what it looked like.

"Where are you going?" she asked me.

"I told you this morning—bowling."

"Well you can't go, I'm making chicken."

Given the quality of my wife's chicken, I was tempted to stay home. But I'd come too far as an Asshole to cave. "I have to," I said. "I bought a new glove."

She seemed surprised by my tone. "What am I going to do with this chicken?"

"Wrap it up," I said, and went out.

I have heard the theory that we are the company we keep. This terrifies me. Probably because the company I keep is a bunch of castrating feminists (my wife, my mom), shallow corporate shills (at work), and bitter lost souls with the nagging feeling they peaked sometime during junior year of high school, probably because they did (my friends).

In this last group were two guys I saw from time to time. I'll call them Brad and Ben, although their names are Frank and Fred. We went bowling at one of the few bowling alleys left in Manhattan, Bowl-Mor Lanes near Union Square, which featured glow-in-the-dark singles bowling on the nights Gloria had strictly forbidden me to go. Tonight was not one of those nights. I met my friends on the street outside Bowl-Mor, and we made our way to the lane and started in on the first frame.

"I have a question for you," I said, after I'd knocked down a pin on the end with my second ball.

"Hold on," said Brad, who took the floor.

I sat next to Ben, who was keeping score using a random method he invented that nonetheless always had him losing. He was about the most negative person I'd ever met, so negative he looped all the way past being a downer and turned into a kind of uplifting comic character. One time I'd told him I was disappointed by one of the people who worked for me, and he said,

"What does it matter, Manhattan's going to be completely underwater soon anyway."

See what I mean?

"Are you happy?" I asked Ben.

He didn't look up. Tonight he was wearing a blue bowling shirt with the name RANDOLPH stitched on a pocket. "I'm losing again," he said, "I'm not happy."

"No—I mean, with your life?"

Now he looked up, alarm in his orbs. "What the fuck? Are you going Jehovah's Witness on us?"

"You think you'll ever make money? Real money?"

"Not a chance of that, dude. *Fuck!—you're on fire big man!*" he yelled at Brad, who was a strong bowler and often hit at least a spare. "Watch me completely miss the pins," Ben said, and got up to fulfill his own prophecy.

Brad joined me at the bench. He had on the nice blue chinos he wore to work, even though he worked in his bedroom producing websites he insisted were not pornography but rather "adult modular content."

I waited till he'd finished his second beer, then I asked him: "Do you think nice guys finish last? Is that true?"

"Depends."

"On what?"

"Combination of things."

"Like?"

"Well," he mused. "The ball weight. Their follow-through. Where they place their feet."

Brad was a man of few words, and beer made him even less talkative. He was like the two most boring people you will ever meet. And like many very dull people, he was good-looking.

"Do you think I'm too nice?" I asked him.

"It'd be *nice* if you took your turn now."

Ben's pessimism combined with his strange score-keeping ensured he always lost, as I've said, so this nice guy (i.e., me) invariably came in second. Brad always won, but this gave him little satisfaction.

We sat in an orange booth near the floor and ate 'tater skins and shrimp dumplings.

"What's wrong, Marty?" Brad asked.

"What isn't?" said Ben.

I told them about my evaluation at work and how I was trying to get more aggressive. Then I mentioned Tina and Dr. Strong, as well as my researches into the Nemesis and his archetype.

By the time I was done, my two friends had stopped eating, had each pounded like six beers for strength, and were staring at me like I had just told them I was the real Princess Anastasia.

After I reassured them I was still the lovable CBM they'd always known, Ben shook his head. "It's a worthy goal," he acknowledged, "but I don't think it's gonna work. First off, people can't change, not like that."

"I'd like to change these dumplings," chimed in Brad, "they're like ass—"

"Also, you're way too sensitive," said Ben. "You don't even like it when a girl gets kicked off *America's Next Top Model*. You cried at that stupid penguin movie, for God's sake. There's no way you can pull this off."

"I wasn't crying, it was allergies," I lied. "Look, it's just—I'm forty now. And I feel like I'll never have a nice apartment, and Gloria is going to lose interest in me."

There, I'd said it. It was a tremendous relief.

"I know exactly why you feel that way," said Ben.

"Why?"

"Because you won't. You will never have a good apartment. That's how it works in this city—you can go backward in real estate, but you can't go forward. It's too late. I only say this to help you. As for the wife, you're on your own."

Brad shot him a look of disapproval. It's true nobody likes a Gloomy Gus, especially when they're right.

"Seriously, Marty," said Brad, "what's wrong with your apartment?"

"It's not just about that," I admitted. "It's more like—I want respect."

Ben started singing: *"R-E-S-P-E-C-T."*

Brad talked over him, "Maybe what you need is a different job."

"I don't think it's the job," I said. "I'm always quitting and starting something new and I'm always unhappy and—I'm beginning to think maybe it's me that's the problem. You know?"

"I've got it," said Ben. "I have the answer: Zoloft. It really helped with my divorce."

"What I need," I said, "is a new personality."

Ben squirted some more mustard onto the 'tater skins. "Finally you say something we can all agree on," he said.

"Doesn't it bother you guys you're not rich yet?" I asked my friends. This is a very awkward question to put to another man. It's almost like I'd asked if it bothered them their testicles hadn't descended. "And what about love?" I went on. "Do you think any woman could really love a loser?"

"Probably not," whispered Brad.

"I've got it!" Ben blurted out. "You're talking about a new personality. What about taking an acting class? That's a great way to meet women . . . late night rehearsals . . . *Vagina Monologues* . . ."

As he drifted off into his post-divorce fantasy world, I thought about what he'd said. Between Tony Montana and Ben, I'd figured out my next move.

STEP

Act As If

THREE

"May I say as the world's oldest living teacher: 'Fuck polite!' "

—Sanford Meisner

Nobody said becoming an Asshole would be easy, and if they did they're an Asshole. You certainly did not hear it from me. Any worthwhile change requires commitment, courage, and cash, in that order. Of course you don't feel like being a dickhead just yet. Question: Who cares? Not me. Change your outsides and your insides follow. Act like you know. Fake it till you make it. It works. No faking.

It will come as no surprise to you that I have had about a thousand different therapists, psychiatrists, and social workers over the years. I've spent decades "on the couch," and it has had a profound effect on my personality: It made me even more whiny and self-centered than I was in the beginning. Like every other person in Manhattan with health insurance.

This is by way of explaining why I felt—at this stage in our journey together—further introspection was not the way to go. My whole life was too theoretical; my library was a lot more interesting than I was. Ben had inspired me to try the outside-in approach.

So I bought a copy of *Backstage* and scanned the classifieds looking for an acting teacher. What did I want? Probably a man. Definitely an Asshole. But how can you tell if somebody's an Asshole from a tiny ad? They're hardly going to announce it to the world: "Asshole Acting Teacher—You'll Hate Me!"

On the verge of despair, my eye was drawn to a teacher with a—well, a strange name. At the time it seemed like an omen. His name: "AL PACIO."

I did a double take. Then I looked at the guy's picture and realized it wasn't a misprint. Tony Montana himself was *not* taking acting students. However, he looked to be nasty enough, from what I could see in black-and-white, and his ad said he specialized in "Eliminating Bad Habits."

Those, I had. I gave him a call and left a message.

Two days later a crabby-sounding older guy called me back at work. If he really wasn't Al Pacino, he did a good job of hiding it; I felt like I was talking to Serpico himself. I made the mistake of asking him what acting method he used.

"Fuck fuckin' methods, man," he spat out. "The only thing you need is the Truth. All that other shit is bullshit trying to squeeze money out of your dick."

He was definitely my man. We arranged to meet in his apartment downtown. Then he asked me why I thought I needed his help.

I gave him a little background on myself and my quest.

"Hold on," he interrupted, "I thought you said you're in advertising."

"I am."

"But you're an actor? I'm confused, big boy."

"No—I want to create a character. And I'm going to play him in my life."

There was quite a long silence as I contemplated—not for the first time—what a silly pickle I'd got myself into with this project.

Emily appeared, grabbed a handful of Kleenex, and left.

"It's your dinero, man," he said, finally. "Whatever floats your kayak."

I thought I'd risk telling him a Truth of my own: "I want to be like Tony Montana."

"Who?"

"The guy in *Scarface*? You know, '*Say hello to my lee'l friend!*' "

"Never heard of him."

This guy had to be kidding. He practically named himself after Pacino. "You guys have similar names," I pointed out.

"Huh?"

"Pacio, Pacino. You know. Did you do that on purpose?"

Another pause. I think he was firing up a cigarette, or maybe a crack pipe. "Guess you're right. See you Saturday, man."

Al—as he insisted I call him—seemed to own an entire townhouse in the West Village on one of those streets that look like a part of Disneyland called Olde Europe. It was very lavish for an actor I'd never heard of, and I decided he either had a wealthy boyfriend, a family fortune, or he robbed trains on the side. The answer, when I finally learned it, was a lot less dramatic.

Like many well-off men who don't work much, he dressed like he was about to get on a boat. I usually saw him wearing Reyn Spooner Hawaiian print shirts or T-shirts from ten-year-old tours by Metallica. Not a tall man, he leaned forward like he had a slight pain in his ass, and his hands were always headed somewhere. He had thick silver hair and a deeply lined, leathery face, as though he'd spent too much time on his roof. His accent was definitely old New York, with a flavor of jail.

"So," he said, looking me up and down for the first time, "you're a lot older than you sound on the phone."

"What?"

He ignored the question. This would happen a lot. "You wanna work on assertiveness?"

"Not really. I—"

He interrupted me, which also happened a lot. "Yes, you do."

"Well—"

"You want to *act* more assertive."

I thought about it. "I guess you're right."

He was silent a moment, then burst out laughing. It was a punchy, pained laugh. "Whoa, whoa, boy," he said. "See what I mean, man! How hard was it to get you to change your fuckin' mind? Not! We've got a lotta work to do, little brother."

"But I—"

"Let's start this peace train now, amigo. Take off your shoes."

Turned out Al was all about the Work. In the Moment. And, later, of course, the Check.

Immediately, he lead me through a quick series of face-relaxing exercises called the "Lion-Fist" (squinching your face up like a fist, then opening it like a roaring lion), the "Lip Circle," with distinctly sexual tongue motions, the "Oo-ee Wee-waw" lip stretcher, and some sinus massaging.

"Okay, we'll adapt the usual voice shit for your Asshole character. Repeat after me. When she kicks the pricks, she yanks the banks."

I said: "When she kicks the pricks, she yanks the banks."

"He fucks the schmucks and gags in bags."

"He fucks the schmucks and gags in bags."

"Hand me the gun you dumb stumblebum."

"Hand me the gun you dumb stum—"

And so on. Silly little tongue twisters until my tongue was twisted numb.

"This area here," said Al, running two fingers in a V-shape over the region around my nose and cheeks, "is called 'the mask.' There's resonators for the voice—they're in the chest, back, and here. Most people don't use them when they speak. If you can activate all three, you're a fuckin' genius."

"What kind of voice would my character have, do you think?" I asked. I was very happy to be speaking words I had made up myself, for a change.

"It doesn't matter," he said.

"Huh?"

"He's an Asshole, right? What's he care how the fuck he talks?"

Al opened up his Sub-Zero refrigerator and scratched his balls, keeping both hands fully occupied.

"Eye contact," he said. "He'd care a lot about that. And the placement—where he sat in a room. In a meeting. What he did with his hands—the handshake. He'd take up a lot of space, do the dominant thing. I'm guessing he'd be a guy who understood body language. At least on an intuitive level. Not so much how he talked, but when. Right?" It was almost as if he'd read my notes on the Nemesis.

There was some banging of glass inside the refrigerator and Al squealed, *"Shit!"*

Then he came back into the room carrying an open glass bottle of pomegranate-flavored iced tea, saying, "You've got a lotta bad habits."

"I know that."

"You're self-conscious. There's a lotta tension in your face. It's like a—like a muscle you never relax. Your jaw is permanently cramped. You know that?"

Actually, I didn't know that. I nodded.

"Your voice isn't clean, it's from a place of tension. Your natural voice is probably okay but you're holding it in your chest, not down here." He pointed to his lower abdomen. "Your eye contact is weak—what're you afraid of? Anything?"

"I don't think so," I trembled.

"How're you with feedback? 'Cause I'd like to give you feedback."

Actually, I was just great with feedback, as long as it wasn't about me. But I thought: suck it up. No progress without pain. That's why you're here: You really want to change.

"Can you talk?" he asked me, and I realized I'd gone inside my head again.

"Sure."

"Let's start with the Instrument. You work out at all? This, I'm doubting."

"I used to—"

"What about boxing? DeNiro boxed. I knew DeNiro. He's a strange cat. Real quiet. Terrible skin. Tell you what—this is what we're gonna do . . ."

Al laid out an agenda for me. I'd have to work my body, a.k.a. the Instrument. There wouldn't be any scripts, line readings, scene study—I was learning how to improvise.

He said: "I don't know you, but you're nothing like this guy, the Asshole. Right?"

"I guess," I said. I was sitting on his pillowy chair now, looking out the window.

"It's a stretch. But it's okay—we can play against type. Normally I'd say that takes talent but since you obviously don't have any, we're gonna work with what we got. Okay?"

"Thanks."

He frowned. "Oooh, is little Marty's feelings hurt? I'm sawwy, Marty." Then he barked: "*Actors don't have feelings! Got it?! Leave them the fuck back in your purse!* You understand?"

I understood I wanted a different acting coach. But this bozo definitely had what I needed: a terrible personality.

"I'm gonna have you do what actors do—they get a part's different from them. Happens all the time. I hang out with Nathan Lane, he's nothing like those fuckin' roles he plays. A really sweet guy, when he isn't hungover. See, he's up in a show, he's *acting*. Know what I mean?"

This made sense to me. At first I'd thought of getting an acting coach so I'd be better at faking things, but Al was telling me I could take it a step further. I could prepare a *character*—"The Asshole"—doing everything an actor does to set up for a role.

The only difference was, the world was my stage. And I didn't know the script.

The next time I went to Al's apartment he met me at the door in a white karate outfit with a red jungle cat decaled across the front. He was sweaty from doing something I didn't want to know about. He offered me a Volvic water and led me down the long, long hall into the *Oh, God!* room. That's how I thought of his living room, which was white and minimalist like a snow-storm in heaven but punctuated with luxuriant green plants and a couple big cats who moved so little I wondered at first if they were stuffed.

"Stand up," said Al, getting down to business right away. "We need to move that sorry Instrument. Do some contractions."

I did what Al did, arching my back, then plunging forward like I was punched in the gut. Then we did windmills and jumps, stretched our faces out and scrunched them up, made weird noises and grunts.

Al was shaking his head, smiling. "How old're you?"

"Forty."

"Hmmm," he said enigmatically. "Late bloomer."

He led me in a Meisner exercise called "Repetition." He stood in front of me and said, "You have a big nose." Wait. "Now you repeat that."

"You have a big nose."

"No, no—*you* say, 'I have a big nose.' Just do that back and forth—until it changes. Don't force it. If it doesn't change—don't worry 'bout it."

"You have a big nose," said Al.

"I have a big nose."

"You have a big nose."

"I have a big nose."

We went on a long time. I didn't know what to do, and I was waiting for him to take the lead. I was thinking he enjoyed talk-ing about my nose a little too much, especially because he had a particularly delightful little nozzle, like James Dean's.

After like an hour of this, he said, "You look annoyed."

"I have a big nose—"

"No, no, no!" he screamed, going off into his "cook's kitchen" again. "You respond to me! Be *in the scene*, Marty! You ain't a robot, you're a human being."

I didn't know it then, but that was about the nicest thing Al would ever say to me.

We began again, and I responded correctly: "I look annoyed."

"You look almost angry."

"I look almost angry."

"Where's the fuckin' creamer?!"

"Where's the creamer?"

"Great! Great! Keep it going!" he shouted as he emerged from the kitchen with a tall no-whip latte in a glass.

"You look like you want to punch me," he chanted.

"I want to punch you."

"You're pissed."

"I'm pissed."

"But you're a wussy."

"I'm a wussy girly-man."

"You can't stand up for yourself," he said, picking up a copy of *W* magazine and thumbing through it.

"I can't stand up for myself at all."

"Keep it in the Moment! Don't judge it—observe it!" He put the magazine back on the table. "Your lower jaw is twitching."

"My lower jaw is—" I couldn't keep this up. His observation was correct: My lower jaw really was twitching. It's what happens when I need to say something but my nice-guy circuit-breakers don't want me to do it.

He looked at me, shaking his head as though I was confirming his worst fears about me.

"How're you *feeling*, Marty? What's the *emotion*?"

"Tense—"

"No—that's obvious—no—the *emotion*. The *content*."

"Angry."

"Like you don't care what I think of you, right?"

"I guess."

"Like a . . . dare I say it, like an *Asshole*?"

Actually, I was feeling like he was the Asshole, but I got his point. Maybe Assholes do go around thinking everyone else in the room is an Asshole. Maybe they're just trying to fit in.

He gave me three homework assignments, which I pass along to you. The assignments, to be done more or less simultaneously, were:

1. *Study examples of jerks in action.* Ideally this was from real life but could also be characters in TV shows, movies, books, anything. Study how they behave and how they talk, and any evidence of what their inner life is like. "Think Alec Baldwin," said Al, "most of his characters, except that one on TV. Also Mamet, *Glengarry Glen Ross*, that's a good one for you." You already have a head-start on all this from your observations of your role model and *Scarface*.

2. *Build a biography for my character.* "Know where he's born," said Al, "where he went to school, what his mom is like. All that." This was something good actors did routinely, he told me. "Some of them write *books* about the role," he said. I decided this one was optional; it seemed too hypothetical.

3. *Use my own life.* Practice jerky behaviors in the course of my day and see what happens. How do people react? How do I react? What are the feelings?

"And when you're out there," said Al, indicating the world outside his huge French windows, "always be thinking: What would an Asshole do now? How would he act?"

"When do you think I'll be ready to try it . . . out there?" I asked him, nervously.

He shot me that look of deep disappointment I was getting used to.

"You were ready," he said, "twenty fuckin' years ago."

"I'm happy to say this, man," said Al the next time I saw him. "Even *you* have a touch of Asshole in you already."

"Thank you." It felt good to hear it, even if I didn't believe him.

Al had told me to build up the inner life of my Asshole character by understanding his story—where he was born, what his childhood was like, and so on. Trouble was, I didn't know where to start. My own childhood, while rich with interior drama and violent, pregnant silences, was kind of uneventful. And although my younger siblings and I begged them from time to time, my parents never even got divorced. I always blamed the failure of my poetry career on the lack of abuse I'd endured as a kid.

I made the mistake of suggesting that the goal of all this imagination was to get myself to feel more like an Asshole.

"Nobody *cares* what you're *feeling*," said Al, with some feeling. "Think 'bout it—can you *see* a feeling? Huh?"

"Uh . . ."

"Answer's no. The only thing you see is what you *do*. You hearing me? You're living in your shitcake skull too damn much, Pee-wee."

"Gosh, I think—"

"No—no! You *do* . . . then you *think* . . . then you feel. Seems backward, but it's true. There's something called the— you heard of Michael Chekhov? Legendary acting teacher? No? Well, he talked about this thing called the 'psychological gesture.' Same point here. What he's saying is, what can I do up there on stage, in rehearsal, to create a certain mental state for myself? You've gotta think about your goal—what you want leads to your behavior, what you do. *That* causes feelings. See how that works? Cause-effect, right? You do, you feel—not the other way 'round. Make sense?"

He took three apples out of the bowl on the table and started to juggle them with impressive skill.

"Even Stanislavsky said you don't have to live everything you feel on stage," he said, focusing on a spot in the air. "People are not rational. We get choked up at a Kodak commercial. Look at marriage—makes no sense at all. Waste a ton on a goddamn wedding, then you just gotta give them half your fuckin' income for life when they meet some guy at the yoga ashram and so maybe he has a house on the Cape. Big deal. That's no excuse to rip a guy's heart out of his chest."

I didn't know what to say to that. He stopped juggling and put the apples down. We were facing each other near the big window that looked out on the street. *"Boo!"* he shouted, in my face.

I'm sorry to say I jumped back and, well, I *yelped.* Like a little boy.

"Start runnin'!" he screamed, and chased me around the sofas. I backpedaled like a clown.

"What—?"

"How you feelin' now? Run—come on! I'm comin' at ya! Hah! Faster, old man!"

And just like that—he stopped.

"What was that about?" I asked Al.

"What you feeling now? Angry? Scared?"

"Maybe—"

"Don't *maybe,* Marty. That's all over."

"Alright—yes," I said.

"Yes, what?"

"Angry and scared."

"Good—now which came first? The feeling or what you *did*?"

"I'm not—"

"Did you move away 'cause you're scared—or were you scared 'cause you moved away? Think about it."

What I thought was Al was more confusing than my therapist. And I rarely understood a word she said.

A couple nights later I was in the kitchen watching Gloria julienne some potatoes when we somehow got onto the subject of assertiveness—okay, I brought it up—and I made the mistake of asking her, "Do you think I'm not pushy enough?"

She thought about this a little too long. Then she put down her knife and said, "There's a lot of different types of guys. You're just sweet and thoughtful. It's okay. It's why I married you."

"Well, it's not working out."

She started chopping up some chives into pieces so tiny they were almost a liquid.

"I'm just saying," I continued, "I'm going to be working on my personality."

"What personality?"

Her comment kind of hurt, but she didn't mean it like that. Also, she had a point.

After dinner, I called Al and told him I needed some help bringing my Asshole to life in the world. He asked me to meet him at the closest thing Manhattan has to a suburban mall, the Time Warner Center at Columbus Circle.

We hooked up at the top of the Whole Foods escalator. He was wearing a psychedelic-patterned Bob Marley T-shirt and jeans, and his silver hair had that "super-casual" look that only comes after an hour with gel, a mirror, and a full team of stylists. To me he looked completely ridiculous, like a—well, like an acting teacher. I asked him, "Why'd you want to meet here?"

Instead of saying something, he stared at me, at my forehead, and I felt uncomfortable so I looked away—which he jumped on:

"See that! What you just did there?"

"What?"

"Looked away—that's submission. I was giving you the Power Stare and you gave up. We've got to work on your eye contact, champ. It's not very strong."

He led me around the mall and pointed out men who were doing particular things with their bodies, hands, and heads.

"See that guy?" he asked me. "He's totally Beta. See—he's looking down, he's all pulled-in, not taking up space. Your Alpha Male, he takes up space. And look—he smiles a lot. That woman's got to be his wife. You're married, right?"

"Yup."

"Straight? I'm kidding—see there, he's so Beta, what'd he just do?"

"I don't—"

"He's got the *Fear Factor* chimp face—see that?"

What I saw was a normal-looking guy in a newish Eddie

Bauer outfit holding some Whole Foods bags and talking to his wife. Sure, he slouched a little, but who didn't?

"The *Fear* face," explained Al, "is when you've got the corners of the mouth pulled down and back, like a smile, but it looks tight. See it now—he's doing it again! What a girl!"

I guessed I saw what he meant. But it reminded me of—

"You do that a lot," he pointed out. "That's a regular look for you."

What he suggested—in between mocking most of the men who happened by—was that I perform self-massage to relax my facial muscles. And that I not—repeat, *not*—smile. Not until I could control it.

"Take a smile vacation," he suggested, "for a year."

"But—"

"Have a look on your face like you just heard your pony died. Good, like that."

We had to go up to the second floor, near the bistro with sandwiches that cost $2,000 each, to find a guy Al considered "typical Alpha." He was a man of modest height in a dark blue business suit, no tie, with tinted lenses in his glasses, and a couple colleagues or clients he was lecturing about something. We got close enough to hear some of what he said—his voice was pretty loud.

"AOL," said Alpha, "and blah blah Raymond fuck blah buyback blah blah incremental subs for sale blah . . ."

"This guy's awesome," said Al, and he annotated Alpha's body language for me. "He's got his finger pointed—that's aggressive. And he's staring at those guys, not dropping eye contact at all. His mouth is smooth. The eyes are looking high, above those guys' noses, see that? He's in their space—close enough to make them uncomfortable. See how that one guy's got his arms crossed, over his chest. Defensive. Those glasses are cool, too—can't read him. But notice he's physically relaxed. The other guys are tense."

"I see," I said, not really seeing at all. To me it looked like some Jack Nicholson wannabe boring the shit out of two managers.

Al summed up: "Alpha's *always* the most relaxed person in the group."

"Why's that?"

"He's got nothing to prove. Doesn't need nothing from no one. He just fuckin' is."

I walked around for a while and he had me practice going more slowly, like I was in a swimming pool. Walking with my shoulders down and my chest out, as though my hands were tied to bags of sand. Not smilng much, with my chin out farther than usual, and my eyes at the level of the horizon, or a tad higher.

The hardest part was when he had me stare at people until they looked away. "It's what monkeys do," he said. "You're the big freakin' monkey of Time Warner Center, Chico."

"Don't call me Chico."

"Alright, Zeppo."

I felt very uncomfortable—but he was watching me, and I thought, "You can't hurt anybody with your eyes," but it turned out yes, I could hurt somebody with my eyes. That somebody was me. It was physically painful for me to stare at passersby. I felt a tightening in my chest and shoulders. Then I remembered I always felt that way because I wore small shirts on the mistaken assumption I was going to lose weight someday soon. You too may feel symptoms of panic. Ignore them.

Like you, I had never executed a conscious act of dominance in my life. Except maybe that one time when I made Tom Meyrowicz take the bottom bunk at Camp Okoboji—but then I felt so bad, I gave him my *Lord of the Rings* encyclopedia for the summer, so it doesn't really count.

Here's an assignment: Go to the mall and stare at people. Really stare. Don't look away or blink for any reason. They'll almost always retreat in baffled submission. Now add a smile to your stare—you'll get a different reaction. Women interpret it as flirty, which they may or may not like, depending on whether you're good-looking like me or ugly like you. Straight men think it's odd. But take away the smile and you're like the Terminator. Savor the turbo-power of eye contact. It gets easier, and then it gets addictive.

Later, sitting over a couple Matcha Green Tea Mists with Energy Boosts at Jamba Juice downstairs, Al explained to me what I'd been doing wrong my entire life.

"See, you've been playing low status for years," he said, "and it's second nature. You smile a lot, don't take up much space, touch your face a lot—like that, there. You don't really look at people when you're talking to them but pay a lot of attention when you're listening. Right?"

I nodded, in shame. I tried to look away since I was listening, but this seemed rude.

"It's okay. It works for you. Just there's a difference between being liked and being respected. You can be like a Beta—loved—but not respected. And an Asshole's all about respect."

"You're right there."

"Another thing—assholes DON'T FUCKIN' AGREE SO MUCH! Even if they do. Think: interrupt, disagree, say 'No.' Repeat what I just said."

"Interrupt, disagree, say 'No'—"

"NO—NO—WHAT ARE YOU DOING?!!"

"What do you—?"

"You're following orders, man. Agreeing with me on every-thing. It's Beta."

He stalked a couple high school girls with his eyes.

"You're completely wrong about that, Al," I said. "I totally disagree with you."

"Nice try," he laughed. "But mean it. Bring the people into *your* reality, don't go into theirs. I get the idea you spend a lotta time in other people's realities. Am I right?"

I wasn't sure if I should say yes, which was agreeing, but I didn't want to disagree. So I grunted.

There are a number of adjustments you will have to make to your repertoire—such as not looking downward, not saying "ah" and "um" when you speak, not pulling in your arms and shoulders, and so on. You will have to be more talkative, louder, bigger, more relaxed, more in charge of the flow of conversation, and less willing to listen. You might say this is impossible. At that moment, at Jamba Juice, I would have agreed with you.

SEVEN SECRETS OF ASSHOLE BODY LANGUAGE

1. DO NOT SMILE.
2. Gesture rarely. Keep your fingers open and curved in a claw and, if you must gesture, raise your hands above shoulder level.
3. Thrust your chin out like you went to Yale. If you went to Yale, thrust it out even farther.
4. Glare when talking. When you're pretending to

"listen," look away repeatedly, yawn, look at your
watch, and take calls.

5. Get very close to people, until they step backward.
   Then move toward them again.
6. Above all, do NOT "mirror" what other people do.
   This builds rapport. Try to make your gestures and
   expressions very different from the other person's.
   (Another fun game is to mirror them so closely that
   they start to get creeped out.)
7. Always lead with your crotch, even if your pants are on.

Now you're ready to take it to the streets. Try being an Asshole
on the highways and stores of your hometown, as I did.

It's not so easy to know how someone would act when
they're totally unlike you. But thespians face this dilemma for a
living, and they figure it out. You do have one considerable advantage as you go about constructing your new persona: *He is exactly the opposite of you.* So, as in a mirror image or an X-ray, you
know intimately who the Asshole is not.

Think: How does an Asshole walk down the street?

First thing is he goes where he wants and doesn't pay too
much attention to trivia like WALK signs, ambulances, and other
human beings. If you want to stop, you stop without looking behind yourself first. If you happen to bump into someone there
are wild accusations hurled at the victim, and a swiftly hoisted
middle finger.

You definitely take up more space than you used to, swinging your arms like a Corleone, not failing to hit stray octogenar-
ians. And you have a very slight look of bemusement, as though
listening to a tape loop of tongue lashings you've recently delivered. You meet people's gazes head-on, meaning utmost disre-

spect at all times, while ignoring anything that's said to you, especially cries for help. Or for money.

You defer to no one, listen to no one, fear no one. You're so self-centered it's kind of funny, really.

Here're some examples from my own experience acting like an Asshole in Manhattan. Remember, like me, you'll make mistakes. The important thing is to keep kicking.

It felt good, at first, striding down the street swinging my arms like an ape. Glaring at people. Looking like I thought something was on fire. But then I realized there was just one problem. Nobody noticed. No one was in awe of my powerful aura. No one looked at me at all. And walking against the light, into the middle of traffic, only made me a typical New York pedestrian.

I needed to shift into medieval mode.

Maintaining my loping stride, I pushed my way into a Starbucks on Greenwich across from the St. Vincent's Hospital Emergency Room. There were a few people standing at the registers, in front of me. I didn't have the balls to cut in line yet, so I decided to speak up from where I stood.

"Let me get a skinny no-foam latte!" I said at high volume.

The baristas ignored me.

"Hey—no-foam skinny—"

"Heard ya the first time, dude," said a skinny, latte-colored guy standing behind the bank of espresso machines in a green apron.

"Then what's the problem?" I asked him.

"Huh?"

"Where is it?"

"Chill out."

"You chill out," I said.

"We're switching you to decaf, dude."

"What'd you say?"

He shook his bony head rather sadly as he worked the nozzles. Steam shot from the silver pitcher like a magic trick.

I noticed, when I paid, the baristas exchanged a glance that could only be called "knowing."

"Thanks for nothing," I snipped.

"Enjoy your day, sir."

I'd actually wanted to sit and drink my beverage, but I felt uncomfortable now, so I went out onto the street, but then I realized that's exactly what an Asshole would *never* do—feel discomfort around people he'd offended—so I went back inside and took a seat. I glared at the baristas once or twice.

They were busy with all the other people in the world. But I was pretty sure I'd made my point.

I tried to make the same point again and again over the next few days as I went about my so-called life. Do what an actor does: Imagine what the day-to-day is for your Asshole, how he would react to major tragedies like losing a shirt button or encountering a rubbery omelette. Be like an actor, only less polite.

Next I went into a CD store we'll call CD Explosion. I picked out a copy of the latest work by an artist I absolutely despise. I won't be all negative by mentioning his name here, except to say that his name is Josh Groban. If you don't know who I'm talking about, please change lives with me. If you do know who he is you'll agree violently with what I decided to do next.

I paid for the CD, took my bag and receipt and left the store. This was only the beginning. Ambling over to the nearest street trash container, I tossed in the receipt and bag, unwrapped my Groban CD—an action I hope never to repeat in my life—and went back into CD Explosion. There was, of course, a line at the one working register.

When it was my turn, I waved the jewel case at the startled witchling in the black baseball cap behind the register and said: "I need my money back. This CD sucks."

She tried the first Asshole-deflection tactic: ignoring me. "Next guest," she said to the person behind me.

Assertiveness guides and coaches tell you to pretend to be a "broken record" when you want something, repeating the same claim over and over until somebody hears you. That's what I did: "I need my money back. This CD sucks."

She relented, sighing, "Okay, give me the receipt."

"I don't have it," I said. "No receipt."

"You just left here," she said with genuine amazement. "Just a second ago."

"I need my money back," I said. "This CD sucks."

"Where'd you put it?"

"I need my money back. This—"

"What'd you expect," said some punk from the line I was holding up. "It's Josh Groban."

"Amen to that, brother," I said, then turned back to the witchling. "I need my—"

"I can't do it without a receipt," she said. "Just go out and find it."

"No receipt," I persisted. "I need my money back. This CD su—"

By now a slight-figured guy in a blazer had come up—summoned by a secret signal. He interrupted me: "I can help you *over here,* sir."

Since he was only about one foot to my right, I didn't quite understand what he meant by "over here." As soon as he grabbed my upper arm and ushered me away from the register I realized he meant something like "away from the sane people."

At a safe distance, he explained to me that he was very happy to refund or exchange my purchase—even opened, as it was—but there was one small and regrettable technicality we'd have to work with. Namely, he needed a receipt.

I stomped out of there the enraged owner of a new Josh Groban CD.

A few days later, I was walking around Murray Hill and I bumped into someone. I mean that literally—I slammed into him on the street. Some might say I did it on purpose. He was not a huge man, about my size, in a pricey black wool overcoat.

Of course, I did not say "Excuse me." I glowered at him. "Out of my way," I said with my eyes. "What the fuck!" he shouted. "What's your problem?"

I didn't fall to my knees quickly enough, apparently. He poked me in the chest, screaming: *"Watch where you're going! What the fuck is wrong with you! Are you fucking kidding me—!"*

How did these people do it? Everyone else seemed to have mastered Assholism. What was wrong with me? I minced a rapid retreat away from this psycho, mumbling apologies until he was well out of earshot.

To my credit, I refused to give up.

Another equally impressive thing I did that weekend was take my lunch into church. It wasn't a church I'd been to before, and I just set my #3 with large fries and coke on one of the pews in the back and settled in to munch and enjoy the service. I skipped communion; I just wasn't that hungry, frankly.

Although a few of my fellow sinners turned around and evil-eyed me during the proceedings, I let it roll off my back. As I was leaving, the minister appeared from somewhere, pointing to the wrappers I had every intention of leaving right there in the pew.

He was a large avuncular man with a white beard and big smile, just like you'd expect. And his voice was deep. "That looks tasty," he said, holding my hand in his. "What's your name, son?"

"Martin," I said.

"I haven't seen you here before, have I, Martin?"

"This is my first time at this location."

"It's so great to have you with us," he said. "Please—and I mean this sincerely—please come back. There's always a place for you here."

I flounced off—turns out I'd ordered a #3 with side of guilt.

You might look over these field tests and declare "Failure!" I, however, felt encouraged. The reason was more one of personal safety: I'd tried to be an Asshole in a so-called tough city and nothing that bad had happened. Nobody got hurt, really, not even me. It was a relief to realize my personality was more flexible than I'd thought. I began to think maybe I did have what it took to at least be, if not an Asshole, at least a first-class dork.

Maybe I could even try it at home.

On my way through the lobby of my apartment building, I ran into my neighbor Ramón. For the first time in my life I didn't say "Hi!" and—like the rest of the Borough of Manhattan—he didn't seem to notice.

Gloria and Hola were at home watching TV.

"Sit!" I yelled, like an Asshole, at my dog.

She jumped on me and started humping my leg, an ecstatic look on her muzzle.

"I said sit!"

She reared up on her hind legs and placed her paws on my chest. Then she stuck her tongue out. We went for a walk, and after she'd pulled me around the building at a trot I sat on the couch with my wife, watching a nature documentary on the National Geographic Channel. This was a series about meerkats, which turned out to be mischievous little mammals who live in the Kalahari Desert in Africa and have pointy ears. I really could not have had less interest in this type of creature, but my wife controlled the remote, so we always watched whatever she wanted. Always.

Now I stepped onto dangerous ground. I had tried to think "What would an Asshole do?" as I went about my life—and here I was, watching TV with my wife, certainly part of my life. So I asked myself: "What would an Asshole do now?"

I said: "Can you change the channel?"

"No."

"What about the SciFi Channel? I think *Battlestar Galact*—"

"No."

"But I want to—"

"Shhh—the meerkats are emerging."

We watched them poke their pointy ears out of their little holes for a minute.

I said: "Give me the remote."

"Why?"

"I don't wanna watch this. It's stupid."

She ignored me, so I grabbed the remote from her hand and started scrolling through the channels.

"What the—oh," she said, intuitively realizing what was going on, "you're being more assertive now? Right?"

You see, she didn't know about my secret project to trans-

form myself, about the coaches and so on. I was thinking maybe
I could reveal the new me organically, so smoothly she might assume I'd always been that cool. I had forgotten that she is
smarter than I am.

"Maybe," I whispered.

Then she patted me gently on the leg closest to her, and
said, "Keep trying."

She took the remote back, and we watched the meerkats
cause many kinds of mischief for the next couple hours.

Back when Al and I were going up the escalator to the street after our Alpha-watching session at the Time Warner Center, I
had thanked him and said, honestly, "I really learned something.
How is it you know so much about body language?"

"Oh," he said, "it's my job."

I nodded. "You mean as an actor. You have to be able to—"

"Fuck no," he snorted, like I'd just launched off some
howler. "Like I'd ever get a fuckin' part in anything but a used
car commercial! With this face! Hah! No, I'm a psychologist, a
jury selection consultant."

"But that house you have," I blurted without thinking, "how
can you afford that?"

"That's not my house, dude. I'm cat-sitting."

It explained a lot. He was still laughing at what I'd said before. "An actor! Haha! Like that's even a real career."

"Well," I said, "you're a good teacher. I'm getting a lot out
of—"

"Good," he interrupted, "I'm happy for you. Now I'm gonna
miss *Grey's Fuckin' Anatomy.* That's two-fifty, check's okay."

"What?!" I asked, surprised.

"My fee—two-fifty, American."

As I was writing the check, there on Columbus Circle where all the cars hurtle past like they hate somebody, Al said, "My fee's one twenty, by the way."

"But you said—"

"Two things, Marty. And I say this for your benefit. One, Alpha woulda known the price up front, okay? Two, Asshole *never* pays the quote, he chisels down."

"Ah—like a test."

"Yeah," he grinned, taking the $250 check from me. "Lucky for me you ain't there yet."

STEP FOUR

Think Win-Lose

Now that you can walk the walk, you're ready for a stroll into a scary place: your own mind. You can't be an ass-master unless you're ugly on the inside as well as on the outside. Right now you still suffer from a crippling disability—you actually care what other people think. This comes from the false assumption they even know you're alive. They don't. You're too nice to be noticed. This Step is about getting over ourselves, so we can get over on others.

More faulty thinking: There's enough to go around. Hah! If there were enough of anything to go around, we all wouldn't feel so damn deprived. As you'll learn for yourself after you've mastered these Steps, even wealthy people don't feel like they have enough. How could they?

"Enough" comes from an ancient Anglo-Saxon word meaning "Hah!," I think.

The incident with Al and his fee made me realize I wasn't where I needed to be. There were many things I was still doing wrong. This insight got even more pitifully obvious when my boss called me into her office one morning to "talk about something."

It was only after she closed the door and seemed to waffle before speaking that I began to wonder.

"So," she said, sitting and steepling her fingers in a brazen display of *femme* masculinity, "how's it going?"

"Okay."

She smiled but not with her eyes. You can tell a real smile from tension in the eye muscles.

"Good, good," she said. "Okay."

We waited. For rain.

"So," she said, "there's something I'm wondering, right?"

I smiled, with my teeth.

"We need a lot of types here—not just races, but all kinds of people, too. That's what I mean by diversity. So there's people who are really going for it and then there's . . . there's others. Diversity."

What?

"What I'm wondering," she continued, "when we talked about this before . . ."

She let it hang there; she seemed to be having trouble, so I said, "About the selling?"

"Right. But—I had a thought. What would you think about downshifting a little bit?"

"Downshifting?"

"Right. Slowing down."

I had no idea what she was talking about, so I showed it.

"Maybe we could put you in a place where we don't neces-sarily—don't *force* you into selling mode?"

"Like how?"

"Give you a slower track. Respect that desire to keep the stress level down."

I was beginning to get it, and it wasn't pretty. "You mean— the 'mommy track.' "

"Hah!" she erupted. "Funny. No, not that. Just ease the pres-sure some."

"So I'd have less work?"

"Well, no. You might have more, I don't know. But we'd re-spect—"

"How does more work lower my pressure?"

"By taking off the stress about promotion."

"So, hold on,"—here I was having real trouble processing, not just being stupid—"I work more . . . but I—knowing I won't get promoted means I get less stressed out?"

"See, this," she said, nostrils flaring, "is where we have a problem here."

I tried my new techniques—the strong eye contact above the bridge of the nose, pursed lips, head inclined slightly back-ward with the chin out, relaxed shoulders, and both forearms on the desk crossed directly in front of my marathon-running ac-cuser. But even I wasn't buying into it.

"I'd like to keep things like they are," I said. "I'm working on some stuff."

"Like what?"

"Certain techniques. I'm not actually using them yet."

" 'Techniques'?"

"Yuh huh."

"Ah," said my boss, picking up her phone and punching in a dozen numbers.

An overt act of dominance.

As I was leaving, she said to my back—or maybe to someone on the phone—"Got to get into gear here."

I desperately needed a fast-forward, so I called Al and made an appointment to meet him again in midtown. He must have been between jury selection assignments or something, because he never had any problem scheduling me. Probably it's because I paid him whatever he told me to.

In the lobby of my building, I ran into Ramón coming in with Misty. Of course he was pounding on his BlackBerry.

"All you need in this world," I whispered like Tony Montana, "is balls."

"*What?*"

But I'd gotten to him.

At Rockefeller Center, where Al had told me to meet him, it occurred to me to wonder: Why Rockefeller Center? What was he planning? What if he had me do something weird? If only I'd listened to the little man inside . . .

Al came up to me and said: "You got a twenty?"

I gave him one, and he handed me a wad of twenty one-dollar bills.

"Today," he explained, "we work on your second-biggest problem. You want to know what that is?"

"What's my biggest?"

"We'll get there. You want to hear your second?"

"I'm all ears."

"You're oversensitive. It could be genetic. We need you to *get over yourself*. Sweet?"

"I am not oversensitive," I said, swallowing hard.

"Don't worry—there's a plan. I thought of it myself."

What I would be doing today, he explained, was offering random people one dollar to insult me.

"What?!"

He explained the method to me again, told me I could stop when I'd given out my stack of twenty singles, and then said, "Go."

It is not easy to describe just how awkward I felt when first let loose on Rockefeller Center to pay strangers to insult me. Since I strongly advise you to try this exercise yourself, I'm sure you'll find out what I'm talking about. It went against every instinct I had—except, maybe, the instinct for making myself look like an idiot, which this entire project is demonstrating.

There were dozens of people within fifty yards of me. It was a weekend and coolish, so luckily there weren't many NBC execs in evidence. Or any of New York's Finest. There were plenty of New York's Lamest—kids and young people, tourists, some East Village types in army surplus and discount store rejects standing alone, tired swingles trudging by with shopping bags from Saks and The Gap.

As you may know, directly in front of the "30 Rock" building there's a skating rink surrounded by a wall, sidewalks, and— right across 49th Street—that area where people wait every weekday morning for a chance to worship Al Roker.

My Al wandered over to the wall and leaned against it, looking down at the rink.

In a moment when nobody was near me, I whispered: "I'll give you one dollar if you insult me."

Of course, nobody heard.

I glanced over at Al, and he was shaking his head.

A couple shoppers who looked old enough to be hard of hearing walked by, and I said, conversationally, "One dollar to insult me."

One of them looked at me and held her purse tighter.

I went over to the sidewalk, where there were more people.

I said: "Insult me—get a dollar."

No takers.

Louder: "Today only—a dollar to call me a dick."

A couple tourists looked up from their subway map, confused.

Louder still: *"Make a dollar real easy, all you have to do is put me down!"*

They shrugged and went back to their map.

Finally, exasperated: "ANYBODY WANT A DOLLAR, JUST CALL ME A JERK!"

From somewhere, I heard, "You're a jerk."

I wheeled around. "Who said that?!"

Nobody confessed. A few people had looked at me, but they immediately looked away to avoid making eye contact with someone who was clearly on a lifelong bender, or worse.

I saw a group of kids around twelve or thirteen years old, with no parental units in tow. There were four of them plugged into two i-Pods and they had on those baggy leather jackets with the intricate needlework that made them look like extras in *Aliens*.

I'm usually afraid of kids because, well, they can be insulting. But under the circumstances that was a good quality. I went up to them.

"Hey—I'll give you a dollar if you insult me," I said.

"Like how?" one asked me, the Alpha alien.

"Any way you want."

"Why?"

"It's a personal thing."

"What do we say—like, 'You're ugly' or something?"

"That would be fine."

"Then you're ugly."

I gave him a dollar.

Because he was an Alpha he stayed calm. But his friends could not believe me. They pounced like Hola does when she sees a nice used Kleenex on the street.

"You're ugly," said the boy sharing his i-Pod.

"It has to be original," I said, making this up as I went.

"You're . . . you're tall!"

I shook my head. "Puh-leeze."

Another one, quieter, tried: "You're weird."

I gave him a dollar.

"You're baby ass juice," said another, who of course got a dollar. He deserved two.

"You're a penis," said the Alpha, and I told him, "No seconds."

This was getting to the point where I was afraid someone might call the Administration for Children's Services, so I thanked the boys and jog-trotted quickly past the elevator going down to the Sea Grill, ending up across the rink from the big gold statue of Prometheus.

I found a pair of older men. I suspected they were from out of town because they wore hats with jaunty brims and colorful silk scarves. "I'll give you a dollar if you insult me." One said, smiling widely: *"Pardon?"* Definitely from out of town.

My offer did not impress a couple of business guys, who

power-walked past me like they were afraid I was going to kiss them.

Most people tried to wish me away, looking anywhere else. Some *told* me to get lost. But they used words that did not count for my purposes.

Remember: "Fuck off" is technically a command, not an insult.

The whole exercise got easier once I fell into the motion of it, almost like it was a contest to give away the money. It occurred to me suddenly that Assholes really are more goal-oriented than the rest of us. They focus on *ends*, not on *means*.

Business people—the real assholes—were not cooperating with me. Best were younger and older people. One group of three grandmotherly women who I'm pretty sure had been drinking for hours asked me: "Why would we do that?" They seemed very nice.

Al hadn't given me any instructions about explaining myself. "It's an acting assignment."

"What should we say?" they asked.

"Be creative."

"For one dollar?"

"Yup."

"Your nose is big," one said. A dollar for the woman with the Brillo perm.

"Do they have to be true?" asked her friend.

"Just say it," I said, steeling myself for the worst.

"You look old." *You should talk, bitch!* I thought, but said nothing. She got a dollar.

The third one couldn't think of anything, but as I was walking away, she did: "You've got a big ass." Well-earned, that dollar.

You'll find it's the more nearly accurate ones that hurt the most.

Weird. Nose. Old.

Not to be ungrateful, but I felt like people's insults were not terribly creative. *Jerk. Freak. Douchebag.* Even—glory of glories—*You're an asshole!*

If only that person had actually meant it.

It became like a game. One rather attractive woman in a blue blazer and hoop earrings, standing alone gazing wistfully at the nude Prometheus, said to me: "That's a new one. Nice try."

She meant: *That's a pickup line I have not encountered before.* And I said, "Uh huh." She smiled at me, and I couldn't believe how easy this was. My first pickup line in my life! And I happened to be happily married. Where was she when I was twenty-two?

By the time I'd spent my wad, I almost wanted to keep going. I didn't feel this strongly enough to actually keep going. But it was amazing to me how much self-centered fear can disappear in fifteen or twenty minutes.

"What you're doing," said Al, over a decaf chai at Dean & Deluca afterward, "is seeing the world for what it is."

"Which is what?"

"A game. A kid's game."

I asked him if he'd ever tried that exercise with any of his other students, and how it had gone.

"To be honest," he said, "I never found anyone stupid enough to do it."

On the train I felt empowered to have a loud "conversation" on my cell phone.

"What the fuck are you doing to me, man," I said. *"It's not gonna work. I need you to take that schmendrick and nail his balls to the fucking wall and then I need you to fucking pull his tongue out with some pliers. The needle-nosed kind. Yeah. And then find his family and take out their tonsils. I don't care how, use the same pliers—"*

"Excuse me," interrupted some slob standing next to me, and I thought, *Here it is, a chance to show my Asshole skills,* but I was wrong. "Who's your carrier?" he asked me. " 'Cause I can't get no reception down here."

I folded up my phone and looked for an old lady I could tackle for a seat.

You will notice that triumphs are often followed closely by setbacks. No matter. Always keep your eye on the finish-line tape.

I was sitting across two seats, as was my new custom, enjoying the space I'd created for myself in the ultra-crowded after-shopping rush. People glared at me, as usual, but I ignored them and started clipping my nails.

Then an old woman, oozing a desperate smell of dental failure, actually decided to poke me with her umbrella. (It wasn't raining out.)

"Hey!" she said. "Can you move?"

I didn't even bother to answer her.

Another poke. "Move it! I needa sit!"

"Too bad," I said.

"Yeah, for you—"

"Stop doing that."

"Get outta there, I needa sit—"

"*Stop*—with the umbrella already!" I yelped.

"Don't touch me! Somethin' wrong with dis fella! He's touchin' my—" she was raving.

"Okay," I said, "take the seat."

Later, Al told me never to escalate into a street fight, and that's what this threatened to become. Although to this day I maintain I could have taken the old lady, if the other guys in the car had helped me.

"Don't want it no more," she said angrily.

"Just take it," I told her.

"Too late. It's my stop."

It was my stop, too, actually—157th Street. Which made for an awkward disembarkation for all involved. Except me.

After each so-called setback such as this one, I'd suggest you do a quick post-mortem. Ask yourself three simple questions, in this order:

• Where did I go wrong?
• Who is plotting to destroy me?
• Why am I so good-looking?

By the time you get to that third question, you should be back on the road from despair. You have "reframed" the picture. Remember what my Communist Uncle Francis often told me: "There are no failures, Marty, only losers. And you are a loser."

The next day I met Al in front of the big fountain at Columbus Circle, and we ended up walking along 59th Street skirting the south end of Central Park. It was a cool Sunday in late September, the kind of day the population of the island aggressively relaxed on. Al must have very warm blood because all he wore was a muscle T-shirt ripped to show his puny guns, and I asked him why I wasn't feeling the altitude yet. I knew I'd been at my Asshole experiment long enough to see some serious results, but I felt like I was still in the second round with sixteen to go, if I lived.

"What's an Asshole?" he asked me.

"Huh?"

"That's your first problem, you don't even *know*. How can you be something you don't know what it is?"

He continued after a moment: "Asshole's someone who— Put it like this: Asshole's someone who's rewritten the unwritten rules. That make sense to you?"

I said no, it made absolutely no sense to me.

"There's a lot of rules—Look at that"—he pointed to the curb where a woman was getting into a cab and another woman a couple yards along was signaling for one. "Why didn't the second woman just grab the cab?"

"The other one was closer."

"That's what I mean by rules. See? That's not a law, it's a rule."

"She was being polite," I pointed out.

"You know what polite is? It's what people do who don't have someplace to go."

Al said he'd been thinking about my project, and he had an idea to take it to the next level. "You ready for this?"

I said yes, I was ready.

"Yesterday I mentioned your second-biggest problem, remember?"

"Yeah—I'm oversensitive," I choked out.

"Here's what I think's your biggest. It's simple, not complicated."

"Go ahead."

"One word."

"I'm listening."

He made me wait for it. Then he whispered: *"Fear."*

We walked into the park and talked about his theory. I didn't say much—I never say much—but as he elaborated I began to get the horrible idea he might actually be right. Truth was, I was incredibly afraid—not of succeeding as an Asshole, or even of failing at it—I was afraid to really try.

"Don't kick yourself, man," said Al. "It's hard to ch-ch-change. Hard enough to be ourselves, right?"

"How old are you?" I asked him out of nowhere.

"Are you German?"

"What?"

"You're really into labels, who's the boss. I kinda thought you might be German."

"Not at all," I lied. Then I felt oversensitively guilty, and added, "Maybe some." (I'm half German.)

"You're the oldest, right?"

"What?"

"In your family? You're the oldest girl?"

I said yes, I was the oldest.

"I could tell—the oldest does not like to get teased," he said.

We were coming down to the road in the park where the runners and bikes were and he spun toward me and yelled: *"Boo!"*

I yipped, then laughed about it. He had done the same thing to me at his apartment, and it pissed me off more then. "What's that prove? Boo!? What're we, like ten years old?—"

"Listen," he interrupted, "here's what we're gonna do. You ready to work today?"

I said yes.

"You're gonna have to trust me, 'kay? Can you do that?"

He was beginning to scare me.

"I need you to do what I say. Everything I say. Every little thing—cool?"

I nodded, barely.

"Let's warm up."

We were deep inside the park now, and he led me through a physical and vocal warm-up for about five minutes, ending with a sitting meditation. Breathe in. Breathe out. The grass was coolish under our butts. I was wearing jeans and a black windbreaker I used to think was stylish because it was the only thing I'd ever bought below Canal Street, but next to Al in his $200 True Religion jeans it looked like a dishrag.

"You *are* the Asshole," he said.

"I am the Asshole."

"You *do not fuckin' care!*"

"I don't care."

"Stand up."

I stood up and followed him deeper into the park, and so began what remains one of the strangest and—in some ways—most important days of my life.

"Walk bigger," he said.

"What do—?"

"No questions. Just do what I say. Okay? We can stop—"

"I'll do it."

I enlarged my walk, swinging my arms at my sides, feeling as totally self-conscious as I always did as the Asshole. Because it was a warm Sunday, there were a lot of people in the park. We took a path back to the road and made our way alongside it under the trees.

"Big chest," he said.

"Big chest," I echoed.

"Big teeth. Okay. Now say what I say but really loud. Who built this city?"

"Who built this city?"

"Louder—Who built this city?"

"Who built this city?!"

"Louder."

"Who built this—"

"LOUDER!"

"Who built this city?!"

"Good."

"Good!!"

People were definitely put on notice by us. Some mothers pulled their kids closer for safety. A couple joggers gave us a wider berth, though we weren't actually on the track. Nobody really stared—they didn't want to encourage me.

Al persisted: "I am an ugly man."

"I am an ugly ugly man!" I repeated.

"But inside I am beautiful."

"But inside I am bea-u-ti-ful!"

"Don't cute it up—"

"Don't cute it up!"

"Stop yelling."

"STOP YELLING!!"

"I mean it—"

"I MEAN IT!!"—by now I was laughing so hard I couldn't talk. We were down on the road again and the strange thing about my little tirade at the end was that it had stopped attracting attention. Literally no one was looking. It was pretty liberating.

"How you feel, big man?" Al asked.

"Beautiful inside," I smiled.

"You ain't that beautiful. Come on."

He led me away from the road again and onto those paths I can never keep straight, and we ended up on a long open expanse of hills and trees that I knew was somewhere just south of Strawberry Fields, near where Lennon was shot. This hillside's always popular, as it was today, with people spreading blankets out, having little cheeseball parties with their friends' kids. It was a shallow hill leading down to the road, and there were groups of nice-looking people spaced every ten or fifteen yards.

"Everything," said Al, "has to be real loud. Assholes are loud individuals. Got me?"

"Okay."

He moved back a few yards—and I noticed he did that more and more as the afternoon progressed and his orders got weirder. By the end he was audible to me, but far enough so that you might think he was just as horrified as you by my behavior.

"Real loud," he said.

"I heard you."

"Act like a monkey."

He'd asked me to trust him. I sort of did, I suppose. But the thought crossed my mind he was going too far. *Act like a monkey?*

I did it: banging my chest, scratching my sides. Ridiculous does not begin to describe how I felt.

"Run around and screech. I said screech, dude!" he ordered.

I screeched.

"Okay—crawl. Just crawl around and say you're a sorry fucker."

So I was on my hands and knees in the moist grass saying I was a sorry fucker. At first I was looking around for what people might think, but I found it was easier if I ignored the blanket people. I knew some of them were staring and calling the park police, but they had their cheeses, and their kids, and those things had to be more important than me.

"Louder," said Al.

I was a sorry fucker even louder—and I was looking forward to the end of this when I felt a *squish* under my right hand and looked down to see a mound of excrement that could have been human. *"Shit!"* I said, rubbing my hand on the grass to get it off.

Al was enjoying this enormously. "That," he said, "was the first real thing you've said today."

"Eat me."

"That too."

"Smoke my pole."

"Now you're faking it."

Once I'd washed my hands, Al and I staked out the region between Cherry Hill and the Croquet Greens, where the roads all crisscross and there is an army of food carts.

The day was getting a little warmer, and there were sizeable lines at each of the carts, some with angry-looking families. I had a bad feeling about where this might be going.

"So," said Al, as we surveyed the hungry hordes, "how do you feel about standing in line?"

Uh oh, I thought. "Fine."

"And how does the Asshole feel about lines?" he asked me.
I swallowed. "What lines?"

"You are learning," he said. "I could cry. Here's what you need to do." He gave me the instructions and pointed to the hot-dog cart that had the biggest line, like four or five people. But no kids, thank God. I was scared of kids.

I was nervous about this but found if I focused just on the task, the goal, not the audience reaction, it got easier. So I breathed, closed my eyes, counted to two and—

Cut in line.

"Let me get a hotdog," I said, in a low yet forceful tone of voice.

The woman at the front didn't say anything. The others were looking at me closely.

"Did you hear—?"

"Anything else?" asked the cart guy, squirting mustard on my dog.

After I paid and stepped back I did the second thing Al had told me to do. I took a bite out of the hotdog, spit it on the ground, and screamed, *"That's shit!"*

Then I marched back up to the cart, pushing the dog at the guy.

"You're killing me," I said, "I need my money back."

He shook his head. "It's fine. No complaints."

"Well you got one from me. I need my two dollars."

"Sorry."

I recognized his look from my research on body language as one animals use to indicate they are not backing down—it's basically an invitation to fight, or a call on the bluff.

I carried the partly eaten dog back to Al, who was practically wetting his pants with laughter about five yards away.

"What happened there?" I asked him, watching the cart guy move on to his other customers as though nothing had happened.

"Not bad," he said, after he'd settled down. "Let's try it again."

Forty years of habit just came bursting out of me: "I can't, Al. I can't do this. It's wrong. Don't make me do it!"

"Who says it's wrong?"

"I don't know," I said. "People."

"What people?"

"Other people."

"And you care why? You really care? About people you'll never see again in your life?"

"Yes," I whimpered.

He looked at me sadly, drenched in disappointment. "I know it's hard," he said, gently. "You're a good boy." He paused. "Now let's try it again."

Something about that *"You're a good boy"* really chapped my jayhawk, as they say in New Orleans.

He took me to a different cart, where I cut in line again and demanded a hot Italian sausage. By this point I was famished so I actually said it with some conviction.

A twentyish white rapper at the front of the line, with either a sister or a girlfriend, said, "There's a line."

I ignored him.

"Hey, there's a line."

"And?"

"You got a problem?!"

"Maybe—"

Al pulled me away from the cart. A safe distance off, he was shaking his head. "You don't engage—that's wrong. You do not fuckin' escalate. You hear me? Focus on the *goal!*"

"What do you mean I don't engage? Isn't that what assholes—"

"No," he said sharply, "they *focus*. What do you want? A hotdog. Go get a fuckin' hotdog. People try to engage you, they step up, what d'ya do with that?"

"I don't—"

"It's noise. It doesn't matter. You want to get shot or in a fight then listen to the noise. Asshole's not a street fighter, Marty. *You* are not a street fighter. Listen to me, it's not somewhere you want to go. Okay?"

I understood. I did hear. He cleared it up for me, in fact. The Asshole is not a thug who goes around like an idiot begging for a beating. He's just the next generation of go-getter.

"Work on those line cuts on your own," he said. "Now let's go direct some traffic."

The six-mile circuit around the park goes in one direction, so the runners and bladers and so on don't hospitalize one another more than necessary. Al had me jog slowly *against* the traffic telling them they were going the wrong direction; again, he followed at a safe distance.

"You're going the wrong way! Turn around!"

And: "Come on, guys! You're going the wrong way!"

"Mean it," said Al.

"You're going the wrong way, everybody! Turn around!"

"Better, but more—"

"YOU'RE GOING THE WRONG WAY! FOLLOW ME!"

Incredibly, a couple bike riders stopped and looked around, confused. They started going the way they'd come, then realized I was a dope and turned back around. A runner stopped and gawked at me. After a couple minutes of doing this—till my voice was officially hoarse—I almost converted five bikers, two runners, and an old guy walking in the bike path (illegal).

There were also people who told me I was mistaken. But not in exactly those words.

It felt like a session of utter goofiness, and it made me mad at Al. Until I realized that among the complicated rush of my feelings there was one I was *not* feeling anymore: FEAR.

"Grab that taxi!" Al yelled when we got to Broadway—pointing to a yellow cab that another guy, wearing a lovely olive peacoat, was closer to. I ran around the guy and grabbed the door.

"Hey—that's mine," he snapped.

Focus on the goal. I opened the door and was about to get in when I felt a hand grab my right bicep and squeeze it.

"I had it first!"

"DON'T—TOUCH—ME!" Where that came from, I don't know. I think the park stuff had upset me more than I'd realized. But the guy stepped back, and as the cab started up I was surprised to see Al sitting beside me, buckling up.

"There's an Asshole in there already, man," he said.

We got out near his apartment, and he walked me over to Christopher Street to my train.

"From now on," he told me, *"always* be the Asshole, everywhere. It is you. I mean—it's not you yet, but you've got to live it to become it."

"I know."

"Don't go back, man. Don't be Marty. You've been dipping in and out and now you need to take it live around the clock. That's two-fifty."

"One twenty-five," I said, firmly.

"Two-twenty. American."

"Twenty-five dollars. Canadian."

He grinned like he'd just given birth. "I'm proud of you, man."

After that compliment it was hard to say goodbye to Al, but we agreed my time was better spent making my way outside the nest. He was always there if I needed him and had a few hundred American dollars to spare.

So I did it—I *became* the Asshole for better or worse from that moment on.

It wasn't hard. What it took, like anything real, was a leap of faith.

I got onto the No. 1 train uptown to go back to my apartment, and I rode that subway like the biggest Asshole in the history of underground transit.

And nobody noticed.

That night I put together a commuting soundtrack for my Zune. It was headlined by the following timeless classics I suggest you pirate ASAP:

HOLE OF FAME—TOP 5 ASSHOLE ANTHEMS

1. "No More Mister Nice Guy"—Alice Cooper
2. "Bad to the Bone"—George Thorogood

3. "Creep"—Radiohead
4. "Take This Job and Shove It"—Johnny Paycheck
5. "What's That Smell?"—Lynyrd Skynyrd

That night I was moussing and combing my hair and watching Gloria debone a halibut. "Where are you going?" she asked.

"I told you this morning," I said, "bowling."

"Well, you can't go—I'm making your favorite, halibut."

"My favorite is meatloaf."

"Really," she said, almost pleading, "you're out all the time now. How about you stay home tonight, I'll make a salad. *Meerkat Manor*'s on. It'll be fun."

I won't say I wasn't tempted, but I'd come too far to back down now. "I hate meerkats," I said, and left.

Half an hour later the Asshole appeared at Bowl-Mor Lanes and bowled terribly. He also won. If you're wondering how this is possible, you obviously haven't been paying attention.

The answer is simple: I kept score. And I cheated. Brad and Ben were too drunk, or depressed, to notice at the time, although there was discussion about the outcome after the two frames. The three of us regrouped in our usual booth around a pile of 'tater skins and oil-soaked calamari nubbins.

"You added wrong," said Brad, puzzling over the scoresheet.

"It adds up right," I asserted. "You can check it if you want." (Secret #4: Never, Ever Admit to a Mistake.)

"There's no way you won," he said, after he'd double-checked my math and found a suspicious lack of errors. "You blow at bowling."

"Not tonight I didn't," I said. "Obviously."

I'd taken advantage of the fact that almost all night my friends had been having a surprisingly heated argument over who was hotter, Mary-Kate or Ashley Olsen. I'm not sure they realized the girls are twins. And that their feelings for them might be illegal in some states.

"There's something wrong with this picture," Brad snorted, crumpling up the scoresheet and finishing up the fourth of one too many beers.

"What are you saying?" I asked, giving the Power Stare to the triangle above his eyes. But he was looking at the shoe checkout woman, on whom he'd had a crush for months.

"You totally cheated," said Brad. "You lost, and you cheated."

"It's a proven fact," mumbled Ben, "that cheaters always win. It's the law of the jungle."

"Whatever," I said.

"Why'd you have to keep score anyway?" asked Brad. "Ben keeps score."

"I wanted to."

"Yeah," said Ben, "and what about this calamari shit? We always get shrimp dumplings, man. Why'd you make us change it up?"

"The dumplings suck ass," I pointed out.

"Everything here sucks. This is the House of Suck. So what? That never stopped us liking it before—"

"Yeah," said Brad, revving up from 10 to like 15 mph, which was energetic for him, "you're being all bossy tonight."

"Somebody has to," I said.

"What's that mean?"

I looked at my friends, sitting side by side across from me. They were both fortyish, currently single, without even a plant or a roommate back in their rent-stabilized excuses for homes. Their careers were treading water, their shirts were an insult to hangers, and they didn't even seem to feel the panic that was overwhelming me.

I said: "Aren't you guys tired of, like, waiting for stuff to happen all the time? There are people out there who are total douche bags, but they're making waves. They don't care so much how they come across."

"This's about that review at work, right?" asked Brad. "The acting coach?"

"Sort of," I admitted. "But it made me see what I've been doing wrong."

"Pretty much everything," said Ben, under his breath.

"I've been thinking I'd get recognized if I just did my thing. But there's people running around who are—they're not even good at anything, some of them—they push harder. You know what I mean?"

"You're going to try No More Mister Nice Guy for a while," said Brad.

"Exactly."

"You're doing it now," he went on. "And it explains why you're so freaky tonight. Even more than usual."

I smiled, then immediately stopped.

"There's one problem with this, though," said Ben.

"What?"

"You weren't that nice to begin with."

"Yes I am," I said. "I'm really nice."

"No—you're kind of a dick."

This was the sweetest thing he could have said to me. But because I was still a man, and he was a man, and we were both from the Midwest, I did not get up and hug him.

"You're just flattering me," I said, swooping over and seizing the last piece of calamari from the paper plate before someone else got to it.

"Think about it," Ben said. "Only an asshole would even *want* to be an asshole."

STEP FIVE

Practice Practice Practice

Forget Carnegie Hall, the only way to get into the executive suite is to practice, practice, practice . . . being an Asshole. Take your new skills into every corner of your life—your marriage, commute, meetings at work, porn chat rooms, et cetera. Don't worry about blowing at first. You will. Press on. Remember there is no such thing as failure; there are only schmucks who need to get out of your face.

Of all the Steps, this one may be the most painful. That's good. Those decades of niceness have turned you into a rusty-bottomed aircraft carrier: You might be able to change directions, but it's going to take a while. Start by attacking those who are nearby, like your family. Then move on to destroying enemies in your village. If your vil-

lage happens to be Manhattan or London, well, you're just going to have to get up a little earlier in the morning.

Like me. By now I was confident enough in my language
and gestures, I knew how to swagger-walk like a pimp and purse
my lips like the Queen, and where to power-stare to be a mint
Asshole. But I had a problem.

"What do Assholes wear?" I asked myself as I was thumbing
through my stack of Banana Republic shirts the next morning.

The answer: They don't really care.

So I'd been doing something right all along. I reached into
my closet and pulled out some stuff and put it on. Olive pants
don't really go with a cerulean no-iron oxford shirt, but I didn't
care, right? As for scent, I figured the more the better, and the
same went for hair gel.

"Whoa!" said Gloria as I wafted past her on the way to the
leash. "Did the bottle break?"

"I'm rolling it out today. For real."

"Rolling what out? What are you talking about?"

"If I told you," I said, fixing her with a plaintive eye-lock,
"you wouldn't believe me."

"What I believe," she said, "is there's something weird in
your hair. Or you forgot to wash it, right?"

"Very funny."

"I wasn't jok—"

Hola needed to be walked, so I saddled her up and told her
in no uncertain terms to behave herself, or else. She told me
that she had no problem doing that as long as there were treats
involved, and plenty of them. So I gave her a treat, and we
stopped by her girlfriend Misty's door, as usual.

Misty's dad, Ramón, was on the phone, of course. He didn't

even look at me as he pushed his baby out the door and pulled it shut.

Or rather, tried to—because today, as you know, was a new day. I shoved my foot into the door's path to stop it. This got Ramón's attention.

"We need to talk about Misty," I said to him, executing what would have been a perfect Power Stare if Ramón hadn't by now turned away from me to continue his critically important conversation.

"*. . . match the color of the wallpaper,*" I heard him say, " *'cause there's a pink rose pattern in the bedroom . . .*"

I stepped into his apartment. Hola and Misty, sensing the gravity of the moment, sat politely out in the hallway. Oh, who am I kidding—they were engaged in a doggie deathmatch, wrestling one another into total submission. But at least they weren't barking.

Keeping up my momentum, I took hold of Ramón's arm and spun him around.

"Hey?!" he said. "Whassup?" He pointed to the cell phone nestled on his shoulder. "I'm on a call."

I said: "I am not walking your dog anymore."

He looked at me like I'd just announced I was a rodent the size of the Ritz. "What?!"

"I'm not walking Misty. Ever again."

I pulled Misty inside, wedging Hola on the other side of the door, and handed her leash to Ramón. He took it.

"And I'd suggest you get her trained," I said. "She's a real bee-atch. Later."

I walked out and shut the door behind me. I won't say my heart wasn't racing—I won't say Hola wasn't a little disappointed—but by the time we got down to the lobby, we were both feeling liberated.

Or something like that.

"We'll find you a better girlfriend," I told Hola during our stroll up Riverside Drive. She only dive-bombed once, for something that looked like a fossilized pterodactyl, and later she stood up on her back legs and peered over the stone fence above the Henry Hudson Parkway, gazing out over the fudge-brown Hudson River at Fort Lee and Hoboken. She looked like a hairy little person.

"That's New Jersey," I told her. "There's a lot of mixed-breed dogs over there."

She sneezed, and I blamed New Jersey. In retrospect maybe it was my six-gallon love-bath of Halston Z-14.

I rolled into Twin Donut imitating a man whose masculinity is so powerful he warps space-time around him. Two enormous hombres stood at the counter, staring sadly at the barren donut shelves. Of course, nobody was behind the counter.

Fording my way through fallen napkins and dirty crumb piles, I went to the back of the store, lifted the vertical folding gate, and roamed into the kitchen area. Four men stood mid-conversation. Metal racks of fresh donuts—literally hundreds upon hundreds of the best-smelling plops of lard and Boston crème in the barrio—crowded the walls.

One of the employees, I remember, wore a bandana. Another—my little morning antagonist—leaned against his dry mop. I directed my comments at him, pointing directly at his chest.

"We're waiting out here. What's your problem? There's people waiting."

"Ah?" he wondered.

"What's your problem? Are you dumb?—"

He was shaking his head, saying, "What is that? Bum?"

"Dumb."

"Hum?"

"Dumb!"

"Huh?"

"Look—which one of you's the manager?"

They looked at one another, not quite antagonistic to me, like they were worried I might be some kind of city inspector.

"I'm the morning manager," said the guy with the bandana. "What's your problem?"

"Nobody's working here, is my problem."

"Cool down—"

"And this guy," knife-pointing at the mop guy, "gets my muffin wrong every morning. I always get the same thing—corn muffin, large coffee—*he can't get it right!* What's so hard? An idiot could do it."

"He gets your order wrong?"

"Every day," I said. "It's amazing!"

"He's messing with you, maybe."

The little mop guy started nodding furiously, almost happily, at this.

"Yeah, I'm messing with you," he said.

I couldn't believe this.

"Why?" I asked. "What's the point of that?"

"I don't know."

"You have got to stop," I said.

"Okay."

He seemed like he meant it. This was not the Twin Donut revenge scene I had imagined. *That* scene had me tearing the whole store a new one, uncorking a carton or two of pure whoopass, and presiding over a ritual stripping of the little man's Twin Donut epaulets before I ran him out onto the sidewalk in tears. But if the way it happened got me what I wanted it was a success, right?

"I want to report you to the manager," I said.

"Okay," said the guy with the bandana, "he's reported. You shouldn't be back here."

The little guy left his mop in back and got my order.

"Have a nice day," he said, as I left the store with my paper bag, "or not."

Even though there was something crunchy in it I didn't want to think about, that was probably the most satisfying corn muffin I've ever had in my life.

I couldn't wait to unleash the Beast during the course of a client meeting in their territory.

It was a big meeting, lasting four hours. Our client loved four-hour meetings, and *really* loved all-day off-sites. This mystified me, because the documented truth is that only about forty minutes of business gets conducted in any meeting, no matter how long that meeting actually runs. Forty minutes is the limit of the male attention span, unless there's a stripper.

But four hours it was. I suspected our client got lonely and bored and liked pushing agencies around. Another explanation was that as a company they enjoyed setting money on fire and watching it burn.

I was there along with the Nemesis, four clients, and the

EVP of our agency. The EVP was on hand, as usual, for commentary and wisdom; the content was left to the Nemesis and myself to present.

The topic was "Marketing to Generation Z"—or, how to get even younger people into debt so they can never quite come up for air and are forced to become that most desirable of all things, a Customer for Life.

Pointing to some digital shots of kids with gadgets, I said: "Gen Z is not only comfortable with technology. They're not comfortable *without* it. To go out without their cell phone, their iPod, their PSP—is totally alien. It's like a psychic need they have for constant connection with their tribal group."

"I think these gadgets are a lot of hype," said the client, who was simultaneously typing something into her BlackBerry and watching the little screen on her motoRAZR, which squatted on the conference table. "What are you saying?"

"I'm saying—"

"What we're saying," interrupted the Nemesis, talking over me, "is that we've gotta push out to this demographic on the mobile platforms. Even online doesn't reach these—"

"That," I stepped on him, "is the simple answer. But I think it's wrong. They're very attuned to marketing—so mobile platform advertising won't work. We've got to get embedded in their peer group."

"Uh huh," said the client, looking up. The EVP smiled at me, encouraging.

"I think—" tried the Nemesis.

"In fact," I went on, "I'd say we have to give to get. There's got to be an exchange of value here—"

What followed won't interest you—it didn't really interest me—but the damage had been done. I'd practiced what John

Alexander, author of *How to Become an Alpha Male,* called "controlling the frame." I'd interrupted and held eye contact, kept my teeth slightly exposed and my fingers together and vertical. I'd gestured up and down, for impact.

And exactly like my hero Tony Montana, I'd thrust my pelvis forward, ready for action.

After the meeting we went down fifty-two floors to meet our car, which was waiting at the curb. This was unusual. Cars waited for people in other professions—investment bankers, high-rollers, Booz Allen consultants—and, on occasion, our colleagues in Above-the-Line divisions, but they rarely waited for direct marketers. I was moving upward; I was with the EVP.

She gestured for me to get in, and as I bent to enter the long black vehicle my ass became unconsciously self-conscious, as body parts do when somebody's looking at them but you can't quite see them looking. That should have been my first clue. My second should have been when the EVP asked the Nemesis to sit up front next to the driver, "for room."

"So?" she asked me, as we pulled onto the Brooklyn-Queens Expressway heading south, back to the office. It was ten after five; it was bound to be a long, stop-and-start drive. Like. This.

"Hmm?" I said.

"What'd you think?"

"It went well—"

"We need to get . . ." Here she launched into a perfectly articulated to-do list only one of us would remember later. I was noticing the scarf around her neck, which was tied like it took a long time to tie. It was bright yellow and her suit, typically, white. They said her husband owned a restaurant. They said he was fat.

". . . and you really did a great job in there."

"Thanks," I said.

"Really took control. You were on the spot, I know."

"Well—"

"You've grown in the role, I've been noticing, hearing things. Really *rising* to the occasion, right?"

Here she either winked at me, or squinted in the sunlight.

"Thank you," I said.

"Like the hair, too. Really good. Shorter's good. You losing weight at all? You're really looking fabulous."

Okay—this was now officially a strange conversation. Or was I imagining things? Advertising isn't banking, after all. And while the EVP wasn't known for being anything other than totally professional, she was most certainly a "character." Maybe this was how she talked.

"Well, I—" I hesitated.

"What're your plans here? Been thinking about that at all?"

"Well, I—"

"You say 'well' a lot. Know who did that? Ronald Reagan did that—you think he was a good president?"

"Not really."

"I hear you're seeing a coach?"

So far, there were three bizarre things about this dialogue. First, it wasn't about business—rare for a woman so insanely efficient with her time she did conference calls from toilet stalls; some of them ended with a flush. Second, it was about me. And third, how the *fuck* did she know about the coach?

My wife didn't even know about the coach.

"Uh, I—"

"It's hot in here." She took off her scarf and hung it on the little plastic knob over the door. Then she put her black leather document caddy on the floor. Then she extended her arm along the backseat so her body formed a fleshy yet distinctly choreographed backward C with me in its mouth. "Better."

The limo was stopped in traffic, and I looked out at a tinted Roosevelt Island.

"So you're married," she said, looking at my ring. "To a woman?"

"Y-yes," I said. "She's a musician. And she cooks—she's in cooking school."

"A singing cook," she smiled. "Sounds like the perfect wife. You know, I've been married twice. Had to take a trial run."

She was still smiling, and as the car went over a roadbump she bounced a little closer to me in the seat.

After a moment's silence, she said softly: "Are you uncomfortable at all, Marty? What are you thinking about?"

"Oh, nothing," I lied. "How long have you been with the agency?"

She said, "Is it hot in here? Are you . . . *hot*? Or do you want to . . . *turn it up* a little?"

I was facing her now, and her lips and eyes were softer, in a way I'd never seen. She had a playful smile, as an actual friend would. What an ally she could be. She could crush the Nemesis in a second . . .

"N-not really," I said. "It's fine."

"You could go far in this business, you know. Really far. But you know what it's gonna take?"

"What?"

"Commitment. You've got to *want* it. Do you *want* it?"

"Absolutely."

"Are you sure about that?"

"Uh huh."

"Don't be afraid to *go for it*—I never was. I *grabbed* every opportunity that *popped up.*"

She put her hand on my leg, lightly, and tapped it. The car stopped suddenly.

I think I bit my lip. I felt like I'd ended up in a different movie than the one I'd bought a ticket for.

"Tell you what," she said, "you *come* to me when you know— this is what you want. Promise me. 'Cause I'm sensing you need to work things out for yourself."

"I promise," I said. I put my hand on top of hers and squeezed before drawing it back.

Here she definitely winked at me. Then she pulled out her BlackBerry and answered e-mails and made phone calls the rest of our trip. I can't remember what I did besides stare out the window, but I'd learned something in that strange ride.

What I was doing—it was working. And I could push it even harder.

Push it I did, taking my skills into the streets and alleys of my hometown. It went better than last time—much better. You'll find this too, as you hone your act: It starts to *work*. And there's no better place to work it than at the retail level.

There was a CD Explosion on one of the streets I happened to be walking down. It wasn't the same one where I'd bought my Josh Groban CD, but I couldn't help but be reminded I was still carrying that cursed disc in my work bag. I went in and stormed a register. There was a surprisingly middle-aged, ratty-looking male register jockey, and he didn't have a chance.

I flung the Groban on the counter with a *thwack!*

"This chomps," I said, angry there hadn't been anyone in line to cut off. "I need a refund."

"Did you get it here?"

He wasn't going to derail me with this transparent ploy. "I need," I said, "a refund. Now."

"What's wrong with it?"

"It blows is what's wrong with it," I said, "and I need my money back."

"Okay," he said, "let me see the receipt."

"I lost it," I said, looking forward to ripping him a new one right next to where the old one was.

"That's too bad," he said, and gave me the list price plus tax back in cash. "This is one of his best albums."

"Craptastic," I sneered, and left.

As you roll it out for retailers, continue to polish and deepen your Asshole persona in the workplace. What I did was call up a woman I barely knew who worked ten floors away and told her—did not ask, but *told* her—to order me the *DMA Statistical Fact Book*, like, yesterday. Five minutes later she appeared in my office with her own personal copy.

I think she was a little surprised to see mine lying open on my desk.

Later, I tried out some funny business at a jazz club in midtown. Maybe it's because I go to jazz clubs about as often as I get my back waxed, or because it's an art form known to tolerate a few wrong notes in the right cause, that I chose that particular place to act like a jerk. Looking back, I'd have to say there were some strikes against it.

First, it was a small venue, with little round tables in four rows of semicircles facing the stage. Second, the audience was with only one exception (i.e., me) unfailingly quiet and respectful. Also elderly. Third, the artist, when he finally doddered out, was so old he couldn't play his Yamaha grand piano any more loudly than *pianissimo*. Fourth, there was a camera crew from the cable network New York 1 there to record this guy, some world-famous French fellow I'd never heard of.

Oh, and I was there with my wife. And she ran into two old friends at the bar. And her old boss happened to be sitting at the table in front of ours.

I kicked things off in style by cutting in front of the coat-check line. This wasn't as powerful a statement as it might have been because the man I cut off could barely see. He probably thought he was still on the Long Island Expressway. Then I had the server change our table, change it back, then change it again.

"What are you doing?" asked Gloria. "The first one was fine."

"That's not the point," I snorted.

"What?"

"You wouldn't understand."

If a "sinking feeling" can be seen on somebody's face, that's what I saw. "Just sit there," she said, "and don't move. I'm going over to talk to Kris and Chris."

Kris and Chris were a couple of musicians Gloria had known from a previous life. They were harmless. But standing next to them was a slimeball I'll call Spike. This genuine Asshole was one of those supposedly handsome, lanky guitar heroes who was way too old to be wearing leather and hoop earrings but had a strange effect on women. This effect was recently enhanced by the fact that he'd played (badly) on a couple of very dull Top 10 songs. He kissed Gloria on the cheek, and I did not appreciate his enthusiasm. Or the way he snaked his arm around her waist.

I'd been given my orders to stay put, but I didn't like it. As you live out your own version of scenes like this one, always ground yourself in the Truth of the Moment by asking: "What would an Asshole do?"

The answer I got, loud and clear, was: Go up on stage and perform some material for the people. I ignored that answer, mostly because I haven't written anything recently. The next answers I got were: *Take something,* and *Complain.* These were my fallbacks. If you removed taking and complaining from the Asshole playbook, all you'd have left is lying and thinking about sex.

I stood up and started edging toward the camera crew.

And I couldn't help but notice my wife peer over with growing alarm. She gestured for me to sit down, but I ignored her. Spike was boring the group with some no doubt self-obsessed rant.

As I passed a random table, I grabbed some breaded shrimp from a plate. The guy whose order it was looked up at me and smiled. "Have some more," he said, "I don't like shrimp."

"Then why'd you get it?" I asked—and didn't wait for the answer.

I went up to the camera crew from New York 1. They were two attractive young women with dark blond hair and black pantsuits. Either one could have been the on-air "talent." I addressed both of them.

"That light is really bothering me," I said, without a smile.

"What light?" asked the shorter one.

"Right there, on the camera."

"It isn't even on," she pointed out.

"Well—it's—it's gonna bother me. It's pointing right at my table. That one over there, see."

"We won't be taping *you*, sir," she explained. "When François comes out, we're going to aim the camera at *him*. Since he is the featured performer tonight."

The women exchanged one of those "oh boy" looks I was getting to know.

"Well," I said, fumbling around in my head for some way to score a point. "Well."

"Well," said the taller one. "Is that all? 'Cause we need a dry run."

"Well," I said, and wandered off.

That went . . . *well*.

Gloria and her friends were standing at the bar near the stage, close to where the crew were starting their "dry run." I wedged myself between her and Spike, grabbed the bowl of snacks and started chowing.

"Hey," said Spike, "hold on there!"

I swung around, eager to let the Asshole loose on this gigolo.

"Let me give you some room, man," he said. "You look cramped." He edged his barstool to the right, granting me some space. "Better?"

I ignored him and continued chomping on his snacks. Unfortunately, these turned out to be the extra-hot wasabi peas I hated.

"What happened to pretzels?" I said to no one in particular.

Gloria looked uneasy and said, "Hey, Marty, why don't you make sure nobody takes our table."

I ignored her and faced Spike, whose black leather jacket looked a lot more expensive up close. "Are you married, Spike?" I asked him.

"Not right now, dude," he laughed.

"How do you feel about married women?"

Gloria yanked me a safe distance away by my arm and whispered, "Go back to the table. I'm networking."

I stomped back and tried to annoy the couple at the next table, but their hearing aids were evidently turned off.

During the show, which wasn't half bad, I made it a point to shout out suggestions to the band in between sending back everything we ordered. *"Louie Louie!"* I yelled. *"In-A-Gadda-Da-Vida, Baby!" "Stairway to Heaven!"* And toward the end of the set: *"Last Dance! Donna Summer!"*

Gloria kicked me under the table, which I'm pretty sure she'd never done before. She was also frowning, and not at François.

I was proud when the band actually played Donna Summer's "Last Dance" as an encore. At least I think it was "Last Dance." They were an avant-garde free-fusion jazz trio, and they could have been playing anything, including the French national anthem.

In the cab on the way home, my wife said, "How's it going?"

"I'm hungry," I said. "Those shrimp were puny."

"No, I mean whatever it is you're trying to prove in there?"

"What are you talking about?"

"You're acting like a jerk."

"I don't like Spike," I said, getting very little satisfaction from her compliment.

It scared me when she didn't respond. Made me wonder what she was thinking about.

"Do you think he's handsome?" I asked her.

She shook her head slowly, but I don't think she was answering my question.

• • •

You'll definitely be shaken up by some of your experiments, as I was, especially if they involve jazz. You will encounter jackals like that Spike character, gearheads and first-class phonies who manage to fool smart women like your wife into thinking they're not evil. You may start wondering why it's so hard for a nice guy to get noticed by the world of women.

That's what happened to me that night. I pondered the common belief out there in the guy community that women are turned on by jerks. Like most suburban legends this one is not true. In fact, my research has shown that women are not attracted to jerks. They are *incredibly* attracted to them.

At lunch the next day I asked Emily and Eleanor whether this myth had any validity. They were both in their mid-twenties, thoughtful and articulate, so I figured they would probably have a point of view. Also, they had never seemed sexually interested in me. This obviously meant they, inexplicably, were not into my type—that is, aging, married guys with a lot of debt and regrets.

We sat in Kosmo's Diner on Eighth Avenue, and all three of us ordered waffles.

I posed the question: "Do women like guys who are assholes? And—if so—why?"

"Let me think," said Emily, the more circumspect of the two.

"Me too," said Eleanor, surprising me.

I sipped my coffee.

"Put it this way," said Eleanor. "Definitely, you know, the Big-Man-on-Campus type gets the cheerleader usually. We like a man that seems successful."

"What about a successful *nice* guy?"

She seemed dubious. "Well—if that 'nice' comes off as wishy-washy, it's no good. Nice is okay but it's—"

"It's indecisive," chimed in Emily.

"That's right—"

"Guys are nice 'cause they can't stand up for themselves. They don't know who they are."

"And they're afraid—"

"Totally scared. We don't like a guy who seems afraid—I mean, that's *our* job, hah!"

They had a good laugh over that. But I was troubled. "What about jerks? You know, assholes?"

"Define asshole," said Eleanor.

"Like a guy who doesn't care about peoples' feelings—does what he wants."

"That sounds hot."

"Put it like this," said Emily, who at the time was six months into a doomed duo with a business-class jerk. "Women are attracted to guys who know what they want and go get it. It's not so much the *way* the guy acts—"

"I still don't get it," I said, not getting it. "Why would you like a guy who isn't nice?"

Emily got exasperated. "It's not like we want to get treated like shit. But we want a provider. They need to make things happen out there. If they're passive we're both going down."

"And let us," added Eleanor, who'd added no butter because she was still on the dating scene, "worry about peoples' feelings, right?"

"True dat."

It was at this moment I realized that for the last forty years I'd been living in the world as—in fact—a woman.

• • •

Later I stopped by the Nemesis's office and asked what was up. As he was grunting something, I looked around his desk and saw the automatic ammunition had been replaced by a well-thumbed paperback book.

"What happened to your bullet that was there?" I pointed.

"I was asked to put it away. In case a client saw it." He opened up his drawer, which was filled with about twenty different types of over-the-counter sinus medication. "It's in here."

"Where'd you get it anyway?"

"My stepfather," he said.

"What's that book? *The Fountainhead*?"

"I'm reading it, well, re-reading it for like the hundredth time."

"You like it?"

"I love Ayn Rand"—he pronounced her first name *Ay-uhn*, although I'd always assumed it was more like *Ann*. (He was closer.)

"What's so great about her?"

"Have you read this book?"

"Parts of it," I admitted, "in high school. It's a long fellow."

He tapped the blue-and-white cover like some people tap a pack of Luckys. "It's all in here, man. Everything I know about things."

For the first and last time in his life, the Nemesis appeared genuinely humbled. Then he went back to punishing his Mac.

"What things?" I asked him.

He made some noises after that, but he'd lost interest in the conversation, so I started to leave.

"Oh, by the way," he said, stopping me at the door. "Did you hear about Lucifer?"

Lucifer, as I've mentioned, was an extremely lucrative opportunity that had been on hold for months now. It was the code name for a massive youth-marketing project our biggest client wanted to launch, and our agency would almost certainly be invited to pitch for the business.

"What about it?" I asked him, studying his eyes.

"Nothing," he said, also studying me, "just wondered."

"What did you hear? Is it on?"

He went back to his pounding. It was a very unsettling exchange, and I wasn't quite sure why. I'd find out soon enough.

STEP SIX

Be a Fighter, Not a Lover

Every Asshole has two parts: a brain and a body. So far you've been whittling your mind into a razor-sharp point of prickiness. You know how an Asshole thinks and acts. In this Step we turn our attention to the body. Yours may not be a temple, but it definitely deserves a sacrifice. Start boxing. Try an all-meat diet. See if you don't start looking, and smelling, more like an Asshole.

I haven't mentioned my cat much in the course of this story, probably because she's so small. Also she spends most of her time under the sofa in the living room. I'll never know what her early childhood was like, since we adopted her as an adult, but it obviously didn't fill her with a love for wide-open spaces.

Also, she was very judgmental.

One night my wife was out at the cooking school working at a corporate "team building" event, and Ruby the Cat, Hola, and I were watching Animal Planet. Hola loved Animal Planet, especially the dog food commercials. Also the scenes of the majestic African grasslands. But mostly the dog food commercials.

Speaking of food, after I'd had my usual high-everything dinner, I settled on the big chair and Ruby emerged. Making sure the dog was distracted by the Eukanuba bags on the TV, she jumped up onto the arm of the chair and made her stealthy way along it. She kept her big gray eyes trained on the dog, in case Hola did something crazy, like move.

Usually, once Ruby boldly made it all the way to the back of the chair she stayed there, vigilantly eyeballing Hola. But this night was different. She jumped onto my shoulder.

This didn't bother me. As I've said, she was very small, and I barely noticed. Also she was purring. Turns out this was an evasive counter-signal to lower my defenses before she sprang her diabolical trap.

She made her way down my chest, onto my lap. Then she turned around. And—it's painful for me to remember this scene—she started to *poke my blubber with her little paws*. She was kneading my stomach like a tiny baker. It was like she was saying: "You're fat!"

While she was humiliating me in this way, Hola decided to get in on it. She stood up, did a downward dog, and starting running around the chair like some demented pagan. The cat kept poking at my tummy, a demonic gleam of triumph in her owly eyes.

"*Sit! Hola, sit!*" I shouted in my best Alpha voice.

Hola ran faster, knocking over the standing lamp beside the chair.

"Sit, dammit! Hola! Goddammit!"

She changed directions, and Ruby darted back under the sofa.

This might seem like a minor incident to you, but it struck me at the time as a total indictment of my way of life, my body, and my project. I wondered: what kind of an Asshole am I if my own pets can call me fat and knock over my standing lamp at will?

I thought about what Al had said the first time we met, how I had to get my Instrument in shape. And I thought about the image Dr. Strong had guided me through, of my ideal self. This ideal self was not overweight. His cat did not mock and belittle him. Absolutely not.

That night I realized I needed to become an intimidating physical presence, a fearsome creature so dominant and terrible that even my own pets might, on occasion, heed my commands.

In the course of my time at Queensway Boxing Gym on 48th Street I almost got killed, and I was reborn. Here's how it happened.

I walked up a seedy narrow stairway painted with peeling gray lead-based paint, the kind of stairway New York used to have back when people learned how to box for reasons other than physical fitness. Faded posters lurked on the walls announcing cards that were ancient history—including one on which Muhammad Ali looked as young as Jared Leto.

I passed a couple grunting types slick with sweat coming down the stairs. They smiled and said hi. Not a good sign.

But at the top of the staircase, shrouded in the darkness, a young Hispanic guy was yelling into his cell phone at someone.

"You wanna know why I'm leaving! I'll tell you why I'm fuckin' leaving—'cause you're fuckin' kicking me out on my ass is why! You're—no, listen to me—you're—shut the fuck up I'm talking here—" and so on, for as long as it took me to get up the stairs. I turned the corner, stopped, and continued to listen.

He slammed his phone shut, snapped *"Cabrón!"* a few times, then moved past me in the hall, shaking his head.

We made eye contact.

"Girlfriends," I said, knowingly.

"What?"

"Who you were just talking to. A lady friend, right?"

"That wasn't no lady," he sneered. "That was my mother."

Now we were getting somewhere.

The gym itself was about the size of a SoHo loft, with two sparring rings set up beside the infectious men's locker room. Eight or ten broke-ass heavy bags hung in front of a set of dirty mirrors, and there was a small floor space for jumping rope. A few worn-out weight machines hung out by the water fountain.

A big woman signed me in and got me to give her my credit card imprint, and I'm not sure how it was done—probably I was distracted by all the feral energy around me, and the holy Alphaness of my mission—but she ended up locking me into a three-month contract at hideous expense.

It was worth it.

Turned out my coach was the young guy I'd seen yelling on the phone at his mother. I approved. If you wanted an agent who would sell his mother's kidney for a percentage point, then you definitely wanted a boxing coach who'd talk to his parents like that. The only thing I'd ever called my mom was, once, a little late for dinner.

The kid's name was Carlos, and I asked him about all the

women in the gym. The place had a lot of them working out, which was strange considering there was no women's locker room.

"Yeah—it's that fuckin' movie," Carlos said.

"What movie?"

"*Million Dollar Baby,* man, you know that sick shit?"

I said I'd seen it. Had haunted my nightmares for weeks.

"I'm tellin' you anyone's inspired by that movie to box needs a brain replaced. But I got girls come in here, I got guys, they bring their bags from work, they work on Eighth Avenue over there. You leave here feeling good, that's what it's about. So why"—he looked me up and down, skeptically—"you wanna box?"

"I'm too nice."

He laughed. "Yeah—I see that."

"Do you get that a lot in here? People who think they're too nice?"

Carlos thought about it. Thinking was for him, evidently, a kind of physical process; it involved many of the muscles in his face, which contracted and expanded like a storm front. "I get all reasons," he said. "You get the guys wanna feel good, you get the girls. Lot of people, they wanna beat the shit outta somebody. You don't wanna beat up on someone, do you?"

I said no, thinking of the Nemesis.

"I had this woman came in here, like three months, she beat the *shit* out of her boyfriend. Came in here right after, had all these cuts on her and shit. You can imagine what he looked like. I felt bad."

"She probably would've done it anyway."

He said he doubted it. "All the time she's working the bag," he said, "it's like she hates the fuckin' thing. I don't know. What about sparring?"

"You mean, in the ring?"

"That's where it usually happens," he smiled.

"I don't know. When do people do that?"

"Your case," he said, lifting his face and leaning back slightly, "maybe never."

It turns out that boxing gyms are not the right place to look for Assholes. I've run into much bigger dicks waiting on line at the New York City Ballet ticket window. Maybe boxing gets the anger out.

Another shocker: Boxing is complicated. I actually began to wonder if I was intelligent enough to do it. That would have sounded crazy just a month earlier, but there you have it. Take the matter of the "hand wraps." My first day the owner woman asked me what color I wanted—yellow, red, or blue.

"I'll take black," I said, not having listened.

She laughed in my face.

"Once you try black," she said, "you never go back."

The wraps I got—blue, as it turned out—were like twenty miles long, and had to be put on manually by an expert, Carlos. He spent about an hour at the beginning of our thrice-weekly sessions painstakingly wrapping the blue gauze in and out and around some combination of my wrist, thumb, and fingers that was always the same, yet dictated by some complex formula known only to the elite.

And after the wraps came the shadow boxing, which is what it sounds like: fake-boxing, into the mirror, with proper technique. Sounds easy—until the fourth or fifth round, when my arms felt like they were going to flake off at the shoulders.

Once I started on the bag, with a pair of big black boxing gloves atop my blue hand wraps, my muscles started burning like the fifth ring of Hell on a hot day in June.

And these gyms aren't all into politically-correct classroom ideas like, say, not abusing students.

"Keep your hand up," Carlos yelled, *whapping* my right ear. "Cover that up!"

My head rang like a bell for a day.

But I have to say the two most surprising things were the thing about *rounds,* and the thing about my *left fucking arm.*

First, the rounds. A round is three minutes. So far so good. But you go to a boxing gym, everything you do happens in rounds. This includes going to the bathroom. It's three minutes on, one minute off, three minutes on, one minute off, three minutes—well, you get the idea. There's this machine. It beeps two times quickly—*beep! beep!*—at the start of the round, then once at thirty-second warning, then twice again quickly—*beep! beep!*—at three minutes. Then a minute of silence, for prayers, or CPR.

Then again. And again. Again. All night long. All day long. For all I know—overnight, when everyone's asleep, so the Queensway gym rodents have programmed in their little DNA the quartz-perfect precise duration of the regulation sparring round.

Four rounds shadow boxing. Three minutes on, one off, three on, and so on . . . Five rounds on the heavy bag. Five on the speed bag. After a couple months, it's four on the heavy and four on the mitts. Then four on the jumprope—which I always cut to two. I was exhausted. I was always exhausted.

Which brings me to surprising thing number two—my left fucking arm.

Here's the thing. There're two arms, for most of us, and in boxing one is held out and in front of the head and the other closer in, by the ear. If you're right handed, like me, the left arm is extended in front, the body is positioned sideways so the left side leads, and the right arm is near the right ear.

Think about that a moment.

What I've just said is the *left arm* is extended in front of the body. Remember I am right handed. Very right handed. About the only time I use my left hand is sometimes when I'm masturbating, to pretend I'm having an affair.

So my *weak arm* leads. But why? So my powerful shot, a right hook, can thunder like the Midnight Express into my opponent's gut. Or something like that. In reality, it only creates problems.

"You got to jab," said Carlos, the first time I hit the bag.

"Like this?"

"No—the left arm comes forward—*pow! pow!*—like that!" Then, later: "Don't hit so much with the right arm."

"But I'm right-handed."

"Use your left. Again. *Pow! pow! pow! pow!*"—in a flurry of left-handed jabs that I couldn't quite see because I was sweating out of my eyeballs. By now every organ in my body had developed pores that bled out water.

So the short story is that my left arm spent weeks in a state of near paralysis that caused me to lay it limply on conference tables and on my desk at work. I made no demands of it beyond the most essential. It had ceased to be my left arm; it had become my jab.

To you non-boxers, it may not be obvious how this activity

aided my goal of becoming an Asshole. But trust me, if you're living in a world of hurt compounded by the threat of your arm falling off, on top of a never-ending feeling of nausea and a non-stop *beep-beep-beep* . . . well, you're going to become a tad less sweet-natured.

The condition of my arms made it hard for me to pick up the phone. Which made it easier to start executing one of my original Asshole fantasies—to turn into one of those office jerks who are loathed even more than the person who steals the yogurt from the refrigerator. Who am I talking about?

The guy who *always uses the speakerphone.*

I shouldn't need to say this, but speakerphones were not created for one-on-one conversations. As far as I know, they were invented so groups of people in the same room could join in a conversation, even though the technology still hasn't progressed to the stage where anyone can actually hear what anyone else is saying. The Asshole doesn't see it that way. He sees the speakerphone as a great way to avoid the inconvenience of having to listen.

Next time the phone rang, I put it on speaker.

"Hey, is Marty there!" shouted my crazy Communist Uncle Francis, who could have been calling from anywhere. I think he lived on a boat.

"Speaking," I shouted.

"Haven't got rid of you yet, huh?"

"Any day now, ho ho."

At this point, my office mate Bartholomew made a big show of sighing, coughing, banging open and shut his desk drawers.

"What's wrong, you sound funny. Are you on an airplane? Are you going into a storm system?"

While I not-so-gently reminded Uncle Francis that he'd called me in my office, Bartholomew gave up and left, slamming the door behind him. I arose, opened it wide, and nudged up the volume on the phone.

"So what're you up to?" asked my uncle. "Still selling shit people don't need?"

"I started boxing."

There was a burst of static—or maybe it was Uncle Francis having a heart attack over the phone. "I must be high—I thought you said you're boxing."

"I am," I said. "It's incredible exercise. And I'm trying to get more assertive."

This next explosion of static was either a series of landmine tests in South Florida, or Uncle Francis wetting his pants with hilarity. Either way, it went on a little long for my taste.

"Did you say assertive?" he asked, once he'd got his breath back. "Marty's gonna be assertive. What a concept. Good luck with that. Oh, shit. I gotta take this—"

I never particularly enjoyed hearing from my uncle, but after he hung up I realized he'd helped me this time without even meaning to. He proved to me that I have genuine, certified Assholes in my own genetic pool.

Take a look at your own family tree. I guarantee a slight breeze will shake a few of them out.

Despite the boxing, I continued to struggle with the issue Ruby had brought to my attention—that extra roll of fat. I began to call it Walter, because I've always hated that name.

To get rid of Walter forever, I adopted a new eating regimen that seemed perfect for my goals. It was called "The Warrior Diet" and was developed by a former *Penthouse* magazine editor named Ori Hofmekler.

As Hofmekler wrote in the forward to his book on the diet, "Whenever something revolutionary is proposed, society is loathe to accept it. Picasso dealt with it, and eventually won. Einstein grappled with it and came out on top."

A touch grandiose, perhaps, but Hofmekler had mighty role models: the Spartan warriors of Ancient Greece, legendary bad boys with superb abs. His diet was built around what he claimed was the Spartan way—starving all day, feasting on lightly-cooked meat and greens after sundown. Dripping with scorn for today's "very unwarrior-like" lifestyles, Hofmekler claimed that "hunger is a sign of vitality and health."

This is not what my mother told me. But I thought it was worth a try.

One advantage of the Warrior Diet was it was easy to remember. Starve all day; eat meat at night. It might have been harder for me, at first, if I wasn't in permanent physical pain from boxing. My arms hurt so much I almost forgot to get hungry.

And the Warrior Diet certainly succeeded in making me more of an Asshole. Before too many days went by, I was so weak and cranky I would have had to look up "polite" in the dictionary.

I did eventually get into the ring. I did it twice. And to avoid embarrassing myself more than I have to, I'll just say about my opponents that one kind of looked like my father's late father, after he died, and the other was—well, there really is no other way of saying this—the other one was a woman.

We wore headgear, though just by being in that ring in our physical condition we'd proved we had no brains to protect. There were three rounds, and Carlos was the ref, although he seemed to me to be spending most of his time at the ropes talking to this new girl student with a wicked hook and a nose ring she really should have left at home.

"With the left! With the left!" he screamed at me, without even looking. It was what he always told me.

The old guy had a pretty mean jab. And I'm proud to say that he only beat me on a technicality. Namely: I gave up after one round because I thought I was going to throw up. The only reason I didn't expurgate on him was because I was so nervous about the fight I hadn't eaten any lightly-cooked meat the night before.

I was less nervous for the woman. I mean—she was a woman, right?

Hah!

"This should be embarrassing," she whispered as we were getting ready to start round one.

At first I thought she was being self-deprecating, in the manner of some of the ladies I knew, but I could not have been more wrong. She was actually trying a professional-level psych-out. I was determined not to give her satisfaction.

I noticed that her arms were strong, but her abdominals looked a bit flabby. Although she wore a spandex top, there was evidence of self-indulgence. And from the way she was squinting her eyes as she scanned my torso, I was hopeful she might be severely near-sighted.

Jab! jab! jab!—three lightning-fast rounds of ammunition from my mighty, mighty left, followed by a power-hook to the kidney, technically illegal but what does an Asshole care about rules? Picture perfect and quick. Carlos would have been proud, had he been looking at me, and had any of my punches actually connected.

Bam!—she let loose a single jab that hit me square in the forehead.

I'd never been hit in the head before. Until recently I was a pacifist, a give-peace-a-chancer, a runner-from-punches. It was not pleasant at all. I think it removed 1978 from my brain.

Pow! pow! pow! pow!—I was getting hysterical, hurtling punches that only glancingly connected as she danced side to side and didn't break a sweat. She reeled me around the ring and then—*Bam! bam!*—a savage one-two that, despite only hitting me in my well-protected gloved hands, almost knocked me over.

After the blowout, Carlos took me aside. "How you feel?" he asked me.

I couldn't say much, draping my body over the ropes for support. I noticed the woman who'd just kicked my ass hitting the weight machines for a workout that I had evidently failed to provide.

"Tell you what," he said, "maybe we shouldn't spar for a while. Get back to the bags. Work on the moves. Okay?"

"I suck," I said.

"Yeah," he agreed, after a moment, "but that's okay. You can get it. Just gonna take you longer, man. You're not"—he smiled, while coldly breaking my heart—"a fighter."

Twenty minutes later, after I'd showered and changed, Carlos came up to me in the locker room.

"How's it going?" he asked me. "Still feel like you're too nice?"

"I don't know, Carlos. I think I'm gonna have to quit boxing."

He didn't seem all that surprised. "That's too bad. Whassup?"

"I feel like it helped me get more in shape," I said, still wheezing and light-headed from the ring. "But I've got to focus on work now."

Carlos studied me closely, though his eyes had a faraway look, like he was in love. I was seriously hoping it wasn't with me. "Tell you what I'll—"

Just then his phone rang. He looked at it.

"Fuckin' moms!" he said, shaking his head. "I gotta take this—"

The one-two combo of boxing and the Warrior Diet had turned me meaner—but not quite mean enough. My experience was that if I made it through the day without eating much at all (as suggested), I usually overdid it at night. What that meant was I'd have stomach pains, and wake up after midnight feeling the Angel of Death descending through my intestines. Which is good for curbing that dangerous urge to eat breakfast, the tastiest of meals, but does nothing for one's zest for life.

I decided to develop my own eating plan—something I called the Asshole Diet.

THE ASSHOLE DIET™

Beta males eat junk. Alpha males eat healthy. Assholes eat.

It's as simple as that.

My goal was to create a diet that allowed me to lose weight while not counting calories, not giving up anything I liked, not having to engage in nonviolent exercise unless I was "in the mood," not having to remember to take supplements or go food shopping, and filled me with a manic energy that would give me an "edge" at work. Also, I wanted immediate results.

Impossible, you say. I'm a dreamer, you say.

I say: Who asked you?

The Asshole Diet™ borrows something from Hofmekler's Warrior Diet, in the sense that both are looked down upon by the so-called medical establishment and both are for warriors. However, my diet is simpler, easier to understand and to put into practice, and produces quicker results.

How? you ask.

It uses the body's own natural response mechanisms of expulsion, chronic nausea, and crippling stomach pain. Through an alarming rise in the acidity of the intestinal lining coupled with skyrocketing rates of such markers of illness as "bad" cholesterol and toxic liver enzymes, The Asshole Diet™ turns the entire GI tract *against* the very idea of consuming another bite of food.

The result: pound after pound melts away, and you're left with rock-hard bone, sinew, and a distinct, generally repulsive odor—three of the core building blocks of the ideal Asshole body type.

Ready? I thought so.

Who Needs This Diet? You need to be on this diet if you have any/all of the following symptoms:

- Bloating
- Constipation or diarrhea
- Logorrhea
- Lazy eye
- Self-doubt

- Stubborn abdominal fat
- Night sweats
- Yearning

To start, the simple Dos and Don'ts of The Asshole Diet™ are:

Don't

- Count calories, carbohydrate content, grams of fat—or anything else that requires you to waste time reading labels, doing math, caring, et cetera.
- Buy organic, free-range, hormone-free, antibiotic-free or otherwise "free" food that is more expensive than it really should be
- Avoid alcohol, cigarettes, prescription drugs, or anything else that helps you make it through the day

Do

- Drink plenty of caffeinated beverages—at least eight full eight-ounce cups of coffee or the equivalent in carbonated energy drinks such as Red Bull every day
- Rely heavily on artificial sweeteners such as aspartame, sucralose, and saccharine that pretend to be real sugar, and so pretend to give you energy
- Take over-the-counter decongestants such as Sudafed, Contac, and DayQuil, and diet supplements such as Dexatrim, et cetera—which make you less hungry until that inevitable binge
- Tell everyone you "feel like shit" because you're losing weight and consequently need to be left "the fuck alone"

I've divided the diet into three easy-to-follow phases:

PHASE I—CONTROLLED ANOREXIA

The first step in Phase I is to forget about what you eat, and when. No matter what it is, it's too much. The next step is to reprogram your mind so you see yourself as a fat, pathetic slob who is at the mercy of forces beyond your control. You can do this using the techniques of self-condemnation and negative-visualization. Repeat to yourself throughout the day phrases such as "I am really, really fat" and "I'm an obese pig someone would have to be stupid to love." Tape pictures of fat people on your bathroom mirror, dashboard, and kitchen cabinets. Caption them "ME—THE FATTIE."

PHASE II—SCAVENGING

Once you've achieved your goal weight—which should be about 20–25 percent less than what the Establishment recommends—you can move on to Phase II. In keeping with my intention to make this diet as "realistic" as possible for today's fast-paced world, this phase involves *not* planning ahead, and eating on the run (usually while standing), buying prepared foods for immediate consumption, eating in restaurants and ordering from take-out places, and drinking only carbonated soft drinks, coffee, and alcohol. In other words, going back to what you were doing before Phase I.

After all, you've lost a lot of weight through a process of self-induced psychic and physical trauma. You deserve to treat yourself, right? What's a little pizza going to do? A glazed donut or two?

In no time at all, you'll find yourself approaching:

PHASE III—LIPOSUCTION

Diets always fail. There's nothing truer than that. Unless you're willing to commit yourself to a lifelong regimen of careful eating, food preparation, water drinking, and exercise, after virtually any diet you will end up right where you began, and then some.

So let's be "realistic" about it. You're going to need liposuction. It's fast, not cripplingly painful, not ruinously expensive, and—best of all—rids you of a lot of ugly unwanted fat even faster than a divorce. It is the ultimate Asshole Diet™ tool. But in the words of the great Ori Hofmekler, "It's best that I stick to the subject of diet and not become a preacher."

So I'll leave you with one thought, and move on.

Thought: In the end, to a true Asshole it's not about *what* you eat—it's about *who* you eat.

STEP

S E V E N

Become the Alpha Dog

**"Dogs remind us how
simple life is."**

—Cesar Millan

Your dog sees things in black and white—either she's the bitch, or you are. She has an uncanny grasp of the dynamics of power and dominance. In this Step, you learn the evolutionary basis for the ascendancy of the Asshole in the modern world. Or at least how to get your snarling sidekick to sit. Then you move on to dominating less complex life forms, like co-workers.

The human kennel is rife with hierarchies, whether we see them or not. Up or down, top or bottom, S or M—it's a rank-and-file life. To succeed as an Asshole you've got to hijack the structures around you and get other people to bend over and assume the position. When you say "Down," the right response is: "Arf!"

Speaking of dogs, the Nemesis appeared one night at

full moon (or nearly) when I was working late and said, barely disguising his joy, "Did you hear about Lucifer, Marty?"

"What about it?"

"It's a go. Client asked for a detailed proposal from us. It's a bake-off situation."

"When's it due?"

He named a date that was all but impossible to meet, at least for human beings on this Earth.

And he added: "Oh, and they want me to head it up."

I looked at him. He wasn't kidding me. "But—"

"You're totally on the team. We'll talk later—gotta go—"

He was off, leaving me with the terrible feeling my Asshole had failed before he'd even really begun. It turned out he was wrong; the client put Lucifer back into limbo. But he'd scared me. Again.

I realize now that I spent so much time on boxing and dieting because I was preparing for the biggest challenge I would face in my quest, one that made taking on the Nemesis for control of Lucifer look like a cool drink of Gatorade.

That challenge was, of course, my dog.

I had only to watch *The Dog Whisperer* for about ten seconds to know Hola was the Alpha Male in our relationship. It didn't make me feel any better about myself that she wasn't even male. All the time I was studying dominant behaviors and practicing assertiveness, my four-legged Nemesis was there day and night to remind me I was a complete fraud.

So it was with a feeling of panic, and some excitement, I looked down one day and decided I was ready. I could take her on. First, I would learn how to command my furry adversary. Succeeding in that, it would be no great challenge to apply the same techniques to my office-mate, the women who worked for me, and others.

"This is it," I told Hola, driving up the Saw Mill Parkway toward White Plains for her first dose of hard-core obedience training, "the beginning of the end."

She smiled and started chewing on the gearshift.

"Let's just start at the beginning," said Gloria.

There were about ten dog-owner pairs in the class, plus scattered spouses and children, in an empty cinder block warehouse wedged between a recycling plant and a Burger King. The trainer, Mr. German, was a big guy with a floppy manner, like a Saint Bernard, and thick glasses. He had trained police dogs at one time, and he talked like a cop from North Maine.

"So," he said that first Saturday, "how many of you know how to sit?"

I raised my hand. Hola knew how to sit. She'd been to puppy kindergarten. Five times, in fact.

"Great—the Bernese. What's her name?"

"Hola."

"So bring Hola out here and show us how to sit."

I hadn't counted on this. An in-class demonstration. My experience of those included the time when Hola broke a "down" command in order to show the instructor how to do the *bossa nova*. We were not called on again.

Hola pulled me out, and Mr. German slipped me a tiny piece of hotdog.

"Have her sit," he said.

"Sit!"

Hola stood taller, staring at Mr. German.

I squared my shoulders.

"Sit! Hola! Sit!"

A look of incomprehension crossed her eyeballs, like I was speaking a word she'd never heard before. Momentarily distracted by my embarrassment, I dropped the hand holding the hotdog fragment. This was a mistake. Hola was the master of seizing opportunity. She leapt for my hand, snatched the piece of meat, and darted between my legs doing a happy dance. Then—as I scrambled to pull on the leather leash, which I held in my hands—she showed a speed enhanced by her protein snack as she started running around and around me, three or four times, wrapping my legs in a tight leather ligature.

I stumbled backward—felt like I was going to fall over—when Mr. German said, not very loud but incredibly clearly: "*Hola, sit!*"

Immediately, Hola stopped running and sat, looking up at Mr. German like he was a choirmaster. Gloria looked pained.

I was unraveling my feet from the binding as Mr. German observed, "She does know 'sit.'"

"Of course," I sniffed, unable to look either at him or my dog.

"Just not when you say it."

There is nothing more cruel on this earth than a canine obedience instructor passing judgment. Especially when he's right.

"Not when I say it," I mumbled.

Mr. German never asked me and Hola to demonstrate again, but my pooch did make some progress. Sometimes she'd sit when I asked her. Sometimes she'd down. The stay was an impossibility. I began to think she was genetically at fault. Perhaps she had some form of canine ADHD no one had diagnosed. Perhaps she really was, as Gloria said to me on the way home after one of our classes, a "special needs dog."

One Saturday I asked Mr. German about my theory.

"Do you think she might have an Attention Deficit Disorder?" I asked.

"I'm sure she does."

"Really?"

"We see it in here all the time."

"Oh, yeah?"

"It's called being a dog."

"Dogs are pack animals," Mr. German explained to us one morning when Gloria had decided to stay home, where it was safer. "You know what that means?"

He favored the Socratic method of instruction, which involves a lot of questions—or rather, in my long educational experience, a lot of awkward silences followed by the teacher telling us the answer.

"They *have to know who's boss*," he answered himself. "They need a leader in the wild to organize their system. The Alpha Dog's the one that makes decisions, others follow him—it's always a male, sorry. If other males started doing what they *wanted* what do you think happens?"

Silence.

My ears had perked up at the mention of the Alpha Dog. It was the mall at the Time Warner Center all over again, except it smelled much worse.

"That's right, chaos," continued Mr. German. "To stay alive they need a boss. It's literally life and death in the wild. Doesn't matter if they're the boss or not—what's important is they know their role. They need a *place in the pack*. It's genetic—they're born with this. So with us, the owners, they're the same. One of you is the Alpha, that's a given. The dog looks to you to *tell him* who's in charge. And what happens a lot of times, you don't even know it but you've told him, 'You're the boss.' Am I right? You're smiling, Randy . . ."

As our classmate Randy went on about something while both his surgically perfected bleach-blond wife and his Rottie, Sugar, listened attentively, I was frantically trying to get Hola to stay in a sit. She seemed to prefer practicing her routines for Cirque du Soleil—at least the one where she rears up on her two back legs and bicycles her paws at the woman standing next to me while I desperately try to pull her front end to the ground.

"What other animal's a pack animal by nature?" Mr. German asked us.

"Sheep," people guessed, and "horses," "geese?"

"*Humans,*" he said. "So does that mean, you take a group of people, we want to know who's in charge?"

Seemed like an easy question, so I said, "Yes."

"Wrong," he surprised me, "we don't want to know who's in charge." Dramatic pause. "We *need* to know it. Even if we think we're too smart for that stuff."

I was beginning to see where I'd strayed, so many years ago. In some fundamental way I'd overestimated the complexity of Man.

Another time we were struggling with the down-stay command (go down, stay there for ten seconds, get treat; repeat), and Mr. German noticed Hola's repeated jumps up after, oh, two or three seconds.

"What's the problem?" I asked him. "What am I doing wrong?"

He hesitated. I knew from experience this was not a good sign.

"I'll tell you," he said. "You're a really nice guy. I like you a lot. But Hola's got no respect for you. She just does her own thing, whatever she wants. It's like she's a teenager, totally into herself."

And there it was again, the dreaded phrase: *"really nice guy."* I'd made no progress at all. Hola was proving it. "How do I get her to—to respect me?"

"That's easy," he said. "Very simple. All you have to do is—"

At this point there was a *yelp!* from a Shih Tzu and a woman screamed, and he ran over. This was disappointing. I was about to learn The Secret. Although that "nice guy" comment had momentarily hurt my feelings, I had decided to be assertive, follow Mr. German, and demand an answer.

The only problem, of course, was Hola. She decided at that exact moment it would be a funny joke to untie my shoelaces and somehow knit them into her tail in a jungle floral pattern. I was always amazed at her ability to accomplish these feats of dexterity without opposable thumbs.

While I was untangling my shoelaces, Mr. German came back. "What was I saying?" he asked me.

"The Secret of dog training?"

"Oh, right," he said. "It's simple. The way to success with any dog is a *chain of command*. Don't get all sentimental about it."

That same class he laid out more rules of dog training. As I adapted them for my own use, they were:

DOG TRAINING BASICS FOR ASSHOLES

1. Somebody is the Alpha Dog. Make sure it's not the dog.
2. A dog is not man's best friend. Man's best friend is his best friend.

3. Never allow the dog to make a decision about anything that isn't bathroom-related.
4. Grooming = Beta.
5. Dog yoga (doga), pet therapists = Beta-minus.
6. Bark your orders. And I mean *bark.*
7. Make sure your motorcycle is always in front of your dog's; go through any doorway first. Eat dinner first. Vote first.
8. Practice the basic commands fifteen minutes every day. These are: Sit, Down, Sit-Stay, Down-Stay, Come, Drop It, Roll Over, Vacuum, File Taxes, Double-Your-Money, and Poop.

A few weeks later, Mr. German came up to Hola and me while we were practicing walking on a slack lead. By this time Gloria had officially decided I was welcome to try this quixotic dog-training thing on my own. "Maybe it'll help you get tougher at work," she said with her usual insight. "How's our promotion coming along, anyway?"

"It's coming," I said.

Mr. German reiterated to us that the key was making sure the dog doesn't get in front of you, and Hola was proving him right by standing about two yards in front of me and pulling on the leash like I was a milk cart.

"I've been watching you guys," he said.

"Uh oh."

"She's got a thing for you." At first I thought he was talking about our special bond of love, how Hola for all her bad behavior really seemed to glow with an inner joy when she saw me—but no, he wasn't. "She's a smart kid," he continued, putting Hola into a perfect down with an invisible command. "She can do all this stuff. Just with you, she doesn't do it. Why is that?"

"I'm—I'm not dominant?"

He nodded. "It's confidence," he said. "She doesn't get it from you. You work for yourself, right? You're not the boss anywhere?"

"Well, no. I am a boss. Three people are working for—"

"Oh," he said, mystified as to how corporate machinery could commit such a blunder. "And how're you at work? Laid back, right?"

"I—I used to be. I'm working on it."

He shook his head, unconvinced.

"What can I do, Mr. German?" I pleaded, almost whining now. "What are you doing?"

We both looked down at Hola, who remained attentively gazing up at her new idol, Mr. German.

"You've got to believe that getting *your* way is best for the dog. Since you care so much about the dog."

"But I don't want to be mean to her," I confessed.

"Cruel," he said, walking away to pick on another team, "to be kind."

"Cruel to be kind," I said to Hola, who immediately leaped up and darted off to party with a particularly attractive Lab mix named Maxie.

Over the next few weeks I did my best to follow the rules of dog training for Assholes, and we made some progress. Once Hola even sat when I didn't have a treat, but then this look came over her face like she'd been horribly cheated out of something, and she went back to work on my ankles.

"Cruel to be kind," I told my wife one night later that week as Hola slept on top of our comforter, exhausted from her latest road show in Tuckahoe.

"Forget kind," she said. "Focus on the first part."

Next morning, I walked past the guard in the lobby and for the first time in my history ignored him. A small thing perhaps, but I needed to set a tone.

And for the first time ever, he looked up at me and said, "Good morning, sir."

No smiles in the elevators and hallways. Held eye contact. Less strain on the muscles of the face. More time to focus on the task at hand.

Which was walking into my office and—amazingly—turning on the light. You'll remember my office-mate Bartholomew, who wasn't in yet, liked the light off, so that's the way we kept it. Not today. I checked my e-mails and set up meetings in my Outlook until he arrived.

And he turned off the light.

I got up and turned it back on.

He looked at me.

"You can have it off if you want," he said.

"It's staying on," I growled.

I remained standing for the height advantage, and stared at him. He seemed puzzled.

"I thought you wanted it off," he said.

"Yeah, right," I sneered. "Just because you like to work in the dark, I really don't." I didn't add, but probably should have, that it was also weird and more than a little adolescent. Also Goth, and I hated Goths. Also he could go climb a bell tower if he thought I'd put up with one more second of trying to work in a bat cave just because I was too "nice" to turn on the lights.

Bartholomew looked at me like I had just come out to him: shocked, but trying to be corporately correct.

"I like the lights on, Marty," he said. "I kept them off 'cause I thought *you* liked it like that. I was trying to be nice, man."

"You are fucking kidding me!"

"Nope."

"Unbelievable"—*all that darkness, those many months, a misunderstanding?*

In the beautiful bright light I tried to settle back into work, but Emily walked in. She was a smart woman and a good worker, but—this has to be said—she could also be incredibly annoying. Usually, old Marty would sit through her long rambling monologues about how she'd really wanted to be a ballet dancer. But this morning, the Asshole did not have the time.

Emily sat in my guest chair, started crying, and grabbed a Kleenex from the box I'd installed for her (but intended to throw out today).

"I talked to my sister," she started, "and she—she told me I'm too old to be a dancer now and—"

"Can this wait?" I asked.

"—blah blah out of shape. She says I should take a class occasionally and—I don't know—"

"Emily, I can't do this now."

Something in my tone was different, and she finally noticed it. Her plea was so plaintive it almost broke my will: *"Really?"*

Almost.

"Really," I said, indicating the door.

The phone rang and it was Gloria. "Can't talk," I said to her more sharply than I meant to, "I'm in with Emily."

"Enjoy her," she said, and hung up.

That afternoon we all took cars out to the airport for a glamorous-not "Core Skills" off-site training session in Cleveland, Ohio, appropriately nicknamed "the Mistake by the Lake."

I was determined to apply some of the insights I'd gathered in boxing and dog training to help me manage the most ill-behaved animals of all: twentysomethings in advertising.

The training was in our Midwest HQ offices in a tall building right in the center of the city. Cleveland only has one tall building, so you can't miss it. The view was incredible since we were all the way up on the 14th floor, which is very high for that part of the world. I could see all the industrial waste dumps I think they called the suburbs.

Like most training offsites this one consisted of a high-calorie snack, followed by some technical problems with the presentation, followed by another snack and some mean-spirited gossiping, a lame comedy routine masquerading as a lecture by an SVP, a gentle reminder to keep it down in the back, a not-so-gentle reminder, and dinner.

The next day was more of the same, only earlier.

For me the highlight was the Team Breakout session, where we divided into subgroups with whoever happened to be sitting at our table. It was probably good that Emily and Eleanor were not in my subgroup since I wanted to practice before I started getting them in line. Who I did have were Jaime and Roger, to-ken Harvard grads, who had an attitude like this firm was beneath them, and maybe it was.

But for now, I had Jaime and Roger, and a couple young

women from Marketing based in Cleveland. Like all such people, in my experience, they were pleasant, competent, and extremely easy for any New Yorker to push around. Like human
Silly Putty.

We were given a practice case about web traffic measurement, about which it would be hard for me to know less.
However, I sat up straight, spoke in clear and even tones, and
made direct eye contact.

"What we need to do is divide and conquer," I said. "Gretel,
you and Cindy"—I've forgotten their actual names—"work on a
measurement plan. And Roger and Jaime, you focus on how
we're going to execute."

"What are you gonna do?" asked the woman I'm calling
Cindy.

"Just get to work."

They didn't move. It was awkward.

Finally, Roger chimed in: "Can I suggest something?"

"No!" I said, as I'd done so many times to Hola.

"It's kinda hard to execute if we don't have a plan," he continued.

"Impossible, in fact," nodded Jaime, standing up.

"Sit!" I shouted. "Down!"

"Why don't we all do the plan first, then move on to the execution?" asked Roger.

"Makes sense," said Jaime.

"No!" I barked. "Get to work."

Since they were right about it being impossible to execute a
plan you don't have yet, Roger and Jaime spent an hour reading
e-mail while the women developed a plan the guys hated. I sat
there glaring as they improved it, against my direct orders.

However, I didn't call them off because, among the five of us, those two boys were the only ones who had a clue.

My grip on the leash was threatened again while we developed the execution.

"This is what we're gonna do," I growled. "We need to figure out how to get the spotlight tags and the single-pixel counters embedded in the log files and . . . well, look at the log files and—"

Jaime cleared his throat. "Excuse me," he said.

"I'm talking," I said. "So—"

"What you just said, Marty—it doesn't make any sense," he went on. "You can't put spotlight tags in log files. Log files are just reports. That's like saying you want a microphone in your bank statement."

Gretel sniggered, or sneezed.

"Down!" I commanded.

"And what's a 'single-pixel counter'?" asked Roger. "Is that like a really small calculator? I think you just made it up—"

"Look, I'm in charge here," I said. "We need a chain of command. You, stay!"

"Okay," soothed Roger, who was still standing, "you're in charge. But how about you let us do the plan, or we'll never get out of here."

He had a point. But I didn't concede it; that would have been Castrated Beta Male. I just went over to the M&M bowl and watched my pack until they were done.

On the plane, Emily came up to me and said, "I heard your team had some problems."

"What problems?!" I snarled.

"Never mind," she said, and went back to her seat.

• • •

It is well known among people who use airports that they are all worthless. But the worst by a factor of a thousand is known to be New York's LaGuardia. Not only is it built on a swamp in Queens, but its runways dead-end in a chemical river and they're *shorter than average*. No wonder pilots who fly in there like to have a couple drinks before landing.

Which is to say my trip home did very little to soften a feeling of nameless dread that had been growing inside me. I wasn't sure why. But I did know boxing and dog training hadn't done much, in the end, for my confidence.

After I got home, I filled the bath with Epsom salts and Aveda Caribbean Therapy Body Crème. My wife sat on the toilet seat covered with the print of emperor penguins.

She said something but I'd sunk my head under the water so I didn't hear more than a burble, but when I came up she said, "So?"

"So what?"

"What's wrong?"

Historically, I am emphatically *not* the guy who takes things out on the spouse. That is lower than this Asshole goes. But some combination of jet fatigue, hypoglycemia, and frustration conspired to make me less than polite.

"Nothing," I snapped. "Everything's fine."

"You don't sound fine."

"Who asked—" Thankfully, at that moment, the canine mini-Nemesis interrupted me by trotting into the bathroom, leaping up, snatching my $150 Hugo Boss shirt from the door hanger, and settling onto the floor to enjoy her snack.

That did it.

"Hola," I screamed, *"drop it!"*

Suddenly, she stopped chewing and fear crept into her eyes. She dropped the shirt. I sat up in the tub and let the bubbles tumble off my sunken chest.

"Hola," I said, "sit!"

She sat up.

"Hola, stand!"

She stood.

"And stay!" I shouted triumphantly, standing up in the tub and showing the world all that I had to offer.

Hola didn't stay for long, and ten seconds later she was fast asleep on the living room floor with one of my socks in her mouth, but why dwell on the negative? I recommend in these moments to concentrate on just how far you've come.

Putting my slightly slobbery shirt back on the hanger, Gloria said, "Not bad. I'm impressed."

At that moment, for a moment, I was the Alpha Dog.

STEP

E I G H T

Put the "Tame" Back in "Team"

"He moves with single-minded purpose, his body relaxed, his gait even, his eyes unswerving and fixed on his quarry."

—Janet Evanovich,
Eleven on Top

Now you're really ready to unleash the beA$$t. You know how to act and think like an Asshole. You've practiced your moves, been ridiculed, cried like a little boy, crawled into a hole to die, wondered if there is a God, taken a nap, and come out fighting. In this Step, you apply your knowledge of blood sports and canine obedience to that eighteen-round grudge match called your job.

This is the Step in which theory finally gets out of your face and you have to go toe to toe with the bad boys who oppose you. Balls flying free, you're running naked onto the field of glory when suddenly you hear someone saying, "For the love of all that's holy, put on some pants!" No matter. Now comes the moment of truth.

The boss had set up an early meeting in her office the next day, and when I got there the Nemesis was already in his corner. Since I was a few minutes early, it seemed that my adversary had either grabbed some preview face time with the boss or been privileged to a pre-meeting on the topic we were all there to discuss.

The boss wasted no time, asking me, "What have you heard about Lucifer?"

I told her I hadn't heard a thing, which was true. I hadn't even known what I was walking into this morning.

"Here's the thing," said the boss. "The client changed her mind. Again. She's asked us to come back with a proposal in three weeks. It's a competitive situation."

"Who's gonna be there?" asked the Nemesis.

"I think Avenue A, Grey, Digitas. And probably Bain and McKinsey. Gretchen"—our agency's EVP—"wants to see it on the fifteenth. So we've got like two weeks to pull it together."

"What shape does Gretchen want it in by the fifteenth?" I asked.

"Finished."

"Oh."

"And there's another thing—this is very important," stressed the boss. *"You can't talk about it with the client."*

"Why not?" I asked.

"She doesn't want to favor anyone. She's clear on this—no phone calls, no e-mails. Everything she wants to say is in the brief. Okay?"

We both nodded.

"So here's what I'd like," continued the boss.

She looked down at her desk, moving a piece of paper around like an air hockey puck in what Al would have told me was a cluster signaling abject anxiety. "I want you two guys work-ing together on this. And for logistics I want you"—pointing to the Nemesis—"to head it up. Okay?"

This was Lucifer: the launch of a new teen-focused credit card product, and how to get it into the hands of as many teens as possible so they could enjoy the privilege of low credit scores and bankruptcy heretofore selfishly reserved for their elders. It was a ginormous project—the first stage alone was probably worth more than a million in fees, as well as a major career boost for the lucky project leader and a bodacious bonus at the end of the year.

Months ago the boss had said I'd be heading up the pitch team; apparently she had changed her mind. But I had come too far not to try to make her change it back.

"I've got," I said, standing up, "a different idea." I flung my arms around and power-stared the Nemesis—I might have over-done it. But the point is that I did it.

"Here's what I think"—

And I came out swinging, as my friends at Queensway would say.

I outlined a plan where we worked in two teams, one headed by the Nemesis, one by me. We'd put forth our best thinking by the fifteenth and the EVP could decide which team would present to the client. "That way," I wound up, "we get to really dig into two ideas, and she picks the best one."

"I don't get it," said the Nemesis.

"What's not to get?" I asked. "Two teams, two leaders, one winning team. Like—oh, I don't know—a boxing match."

"It's a waste," said the Nemesis.

"Why'd we do that?" asked the boss.

"Yeah—why?"

" 'Cause we"—I pointed to the Nemesis, palm flat and vertical—"don't agree. We have different approaches to Gen Z and—and we won't know which one works better unless we do a lot of work on both. This way we'll drive to the best answer for the pitch—"

"Hold on," said the boss, "what do you mean 'different approaches'? How're they different?"

"We both agree the blatant sales pitches on these social networking sites don't work with younger people—they'd see right through it on MySpace and Facebook."

"R-right."

"But he thinks," pointing at the Nemesis, "we should focus on the mobile platforms and sell ads there. It's still a blatant pitch. I think we have to get embedded in the networks themselves and build a viral word-of-mouth about the products—"

"That's too hard," said the Nemesis, "and it doesn't w—"

"It can too work—kids make recommendations all the time. Look at *Borat*—"

"You don't know that—"

"Selling banner ads on iPods is a waste of—"

"—word of mouth didn't—you're imagining—"

"*Okay!*" said the boss, loud enough to stop us dead. "I get it. You don't agree. And I don't know who's right."

"Therefore," I said, with a triumphant leonine head toss, "two teams."

"*Waste of time*—" whispered the Nemesis—

"*Not my time*—" I shot back—

"Guys, come on," scolded the boss. She made a show of looking through her staffing sheet, but I could see she thought I'd made sense. "You have capacity for your other projects?"

"Yes," I said. The Nemesis stayed silent.

"You can do it with two analysts?"

"Each," said the Nemesis, and I said, "Yup."

The boss thought some more.

"Okay," she smiled, "two teams. Two analysts. Two weeks. That's a whole lotta twos—"

"I don't know," said the Nemesis. "Still seems like a waste of time to me."

"You could always concede," I said.

Before the boss changed her mind again, I left her office and grabbed Emily and Eleanor at their desks. I briefed them in my place and unleashed them to put together a workplan.

Then I called Gloria on her cell phone and debriefed her. I heard screaming in the background—some kind of cooking emergency. But one thing I'd learned about commercial cooking was there was always an emergency.

"I've positioned it as a one-on-one," I said to her. "My team against the Nemesis."

"Good strategy," she said. "If you win this one you're on trajectory to take it all. The promotion, the bonus. Now let's get clear on tactics." We talked for a few minutes and agreed a shock-and-awe blitzkrieg running up to the EVP encounter could demoralize the enemy and make the most of my limited firepower. Having been given my marching orders, I rang off.

A few hours later, my boss called me into her sanctum again.

Without the Nemesis this time, she waited. I didn't bother to sit; she didn't bother to ask me.

"Close the door," she said. "This's something I told [the

Nemesis] earlier, it's relevant to you. Things are kinda slow around here—"

"Not for long—"

"I talked to Gretchen, it's official now we can only put up one promotion this round. There's only one slot."

"Okay." I turned to go.

"Wait a second, you're running off a lot today. We aren't done."

"Yes, we are," I said. "There's one promotion. It's him and me. One man wins. You decide—"

"The Committee decides—"

"Whatever, the Committee decides between us two. What'd I miss?"

"Gretchen wants the recommendation in a couple weeks."

"Ah," I thought out loud. "So it's how we do on Lucifer that decides—"

"Among oth—"

"It's weird I suggested we go head to head, right?"

"I was gonna suggest it myself."

I looked at her and, as usual, wasn't sure what to say next. So I asked myself: What would an Asshole say now?

"No you weren't."

She looked like she'd never seen me before in her life.

So this is where I found myself: two weeks to an internal presentation with our agency EVP, after which she'd pick either my team or the Nemesis's to head into the all-important client pitch meeting the following week. Him or me, up or down, life or purgatory.

I stole the good conference room in the corner, the one with all the windows that's always booked up, and I had my boss's assistant Noemi make up a big sign that read:

"RESERVED FOR D. RICHARD—24/7 TILL FURTHER NOTICE
DO NOT ENTER (This means YOU!)"

D. Richard was our company's chairman, and he hadn't been seen on our floor in about twenty-five years. But no matter; his name had a kind of shamanic power to repel.

"I like the 'This means YOU!' " I told Noemi, remembering too late I'd decided to be an Asshole till further notice.

"Thanks," she smiled, "I think it adds some teeth."

"Now put it up."

I got my two analysts into the room and laid out the playbook for them.

"We've got two weeks to put this together," I rapid-fired. "It's 'Marketing to Gen Z'—now, you guys are Gen Y. So don't think of yourself as the demo you're marketing to—"

"But why not?" asked Emily, who was obviously not here to make my life easy.

"How to put this?" I mused. "You're too old. And too nerdy."

"I'm not a nerd—"

"I am," admitted Eleanor, smearing butter on a warm Pop-Tart. With her finger.

"What are you doing here? Can you stop it?" I asked.

"Sorry, sir," she cooed. Then she napkined her butter finger. Slowly.

I would need to do something now.

"Look!" I said, *smacking* the tabletop with my palms. They

both jumped. "This is serious. There's *no* attitude about this and there's *no* snacking in the conference rooms. Throw that away."

"What—?"

With a controlled sweeping gesture I slid the paper napkin and the Pop-Tart off the surface of the conference table and into a wastebasket at its side. Eleanor's mouth was literally open.

"I need you to listen," I continued. "There's two weeks. I have an idea about embedding into social networks. That other team is off with a platform approach that's just—just stupid and wrong. What I need from you two are examples of how this networking makes itself felt in the market, right? So Eleanor, you look for other companies, products where it's worked."

"What's worked?" she pouted.

"Embedding a message into a community—like a network of recommendations. And Emily, you find out where those communities are—"

"You mean online?"

"Yes, online. But also in the world—"

I went on to describe what I thought our approach should be and what I wanted them to do, and after a while Emily came out with: "Oh—there's a problem. It's my boyfriend's birthday tonight."

"And?" I asked.

"I need to get out, like, at five." She waited. "Hope that's not a problem."

I was enough of an Asshole now in my soul I didn't even have to ponder my response.

"You can leave at five, alright," I sneered. "On the fifteenth. For the next two weeks I need you both here 'round the clock. You can go home to shower and change but that's it. The other

guys are on our ass and they're *smarter* than we are. They've got
Jaime and Roger. They went to Harvard—"

"So what do I tell my boyfriend?" asked Emily.

She was making me angry, and I knew from my work with
Hola it was easier to be an Asshole when you're mad.

"Tell him if you want a fucking job tomorrow, his birthday's
in the waiting room."

"Are you okay?"

"What? Yes—yes, I'm fine. Are you okay with working?"
Then I added: "For a change?"

Both of their eyes bugged open, and they quickly shifted
back in their seats. Eleanor actually looked at the door, like she
wanted to escape.

I let the uncomfortable silence hang there a moment, then
I left. As I walked out, I heard both of them exhale.

I was outlining the Lucifer presentation in PowerPoint when my
phone rang. It was my Communist Uncle Francis again. He
liked to call me at work just to confirm someone was stupid
enough to employ me full-time.

His first words were always:

"Haven't got rid of you yet, huh?"

And my response was always:

"Any day now. Ho ho."

But on this day, as you know, I was a different nephew alto-
gether. And he had selected the wrong day to call.

"Uncle Francis," I began, white-knuckling the speakerphone
in my hands, "how many times have I been fired from a job? In
my life?"

"What's that?"

"*None.* That's how many times. Not *once,*" I breathed in and breathed out, imagining my unsafe space with the portraits of my enemies on the red molten walls. "Now *you've* been fired— that's true. But don't take your insecurities out on me 'cause I used to be half a man. I'm getting tired of this shit with the jokes. So stop with the freakin' innuendos—are you there?"

Bartholomew swung around in his chair and looked at me like, *Who are you talking to?*

I definitely needed to put a priority on getting my own office.

There was a whistling breeze sound on the phone as my uncle processed what I'd said.

But no. Actually—"What's that?" he said, coming back on the line. "I dropped the phone. Did you say something?"

I told him I couldn't talk right then, and I did not add, "because you annoy the shit out of me."

Right then Gloria called, and I told her too that I couldn't talk, I was busy.

"Meeting with little Emily?" she asked me. Sarcasm isn't my wife's usual style, so I had trouble recognizing it.

"No, as a matter of fact," I said. "We're meeting later on."

"Of course you are."

After I hung up, Bartholomew twirled around in his chair and said: "We're having quite the family reunion today."

"Mind your business."

"Whoa—who changed your meds, man? You're all dangerous."

"Just leave it."

He turned and didn't talk to me for the following forty-eight hours, which allowed me to get a lot of work done. Gloria evidently also received the message: she didn't call me at work for a few days.

The Nemesis had staked out another conference room on our floor, opposite to mine. He had no lying sign on the door, as I had, but his two boys were camped inside. I saw them through the door crack as they came and went to the bathroom, coffeemaker, copier, and so on. My team was discouraged from breaking.

A couple times I looped the floor, to gain intelligence, but I didn't see the Nemesis anywhere. Thought maybe he'd left the building for his loft. But on my second loop I saw my boss coming out of her office trailing the Nemesis, and both of their heads were—were they really?—*bowed in prayer!*

Or so I imagined. It was quite late. I could have been wrong.

"You guys praying?" I said, as I passed.

"To Satan," said the Nemesis.

Then I fantasized about calling Facilities and asking them to put up a regulation-size boxing ring in the large conference room on the nineteenth floor for my face-off with the Nemesis.

Emily and Eleanor didn't light up warmly at our eight a.m. meetings, but they were there, prepared, with their high helping of research as requested. We went over the PowerPoint draft of the presentation, and I spent the afternoon reworking it. Then we met again and chunked out the missing pieces.

When I say *chunked* I mean that literally: I spent a lot of time in the bathroom, due to my diet. But I'll spare you the details—you'll find out for yourself, when you try it.

Our Lucifer argument was that we could use behavioral algorithms to identify influentials in the Gen Z demographic and then recruit these influentials—defined as kids with a certain critical mass of social contacts and friends—to shill our products. We'd give them free stuff, and we'd pay them some nominal "consulting fee."

Of course there was the tricky question: What if you found the influential kids, got the product into their hands, got them to agree to recommend it to their network if they liked it and . . . they didn't like it? Were they then supposed to just *lie*? Current wisdom was they should be paid no matter what they said, which was almost impossible to monitor anyway. So more than one company had been forced into the counterintuitive position of paying kids to tell their friends not to buy their product because it, like, sucked.

Here was my idea: We'd pay them to "guarantee referral."

That is, if they liked the product, they'd tell their friends they liked it.

If they didn't like it—well, they'd tell their friends they liked it.

They'd *lie*. For *money*.

"Isn't there an ethical thing here?" asked Eleanor in her young-person's naïve way.

"Like how?" I asked her.

"Like if I had a friend I found out she was lying to me to get paid for it—I don't know, I wouldn't think that was so great, you know?"

"She agreed to do it," I pointed out.

"That makes it worse. It's like we're attracting assholes."

"And?"

"Well," she said, puzzling, "why do we want amoral customers?"

"What're you, born again? They're not *amoral*—"

"They have no integrity."

"What do we do here all the time? At this firm? We lie to sell products. The other name for that is advertising."

"Yeah, but people expect us to do it. They don't believe a word we say. It's different with your friends—"

The Nemesis picked this moment to peek in—his head appeared disembodied for a second, horizontal, and was followed by his body, in black jeans and a black turtleneck that emphasized his scary muscle fiber. "Hiya guys," he grinned, "sounds intense in here."

"What's up?!" I snapped.

"Just sayin' 'hi.' So: 'Hi!'"

"Hi," said my grumpy girls, and he looked at them and asked: "You're coming to my party, right? Friday night?"

This was the first I'd heard of any party, but the girls seemed to know what he was talking about.

"I dunno," said Eleanor.

"Can we bring someone?" asked Emily.

The Nemesis put his arm around my shoulders like a coach, and I wanted to hurl. "You're gonna let 'em out Friday night, right, boss?"

"I don't know—"

"Oh, come on, you know you've got this thing locked up. I'm ready to toss in the towel."

"Why don't you?"

He winked at me. "See you Friday. Oh—and I was talking to Sherry, she might be able to make it. So you should poke your head in."

After he left our team room I went after him, cornering him against a cabinet in the hall. He wasn't smiling anymore.

"You talked to Sherry?" She was the client for Lucifer, the one the boss had *explicitly told us not to reach out to* before the pitch because *she herself had requested it.* I'd never met her.

"Sure," said the Nemesis. "We talk all the time."

"You called her?"

"What did I just say? She's cool with—"

"But she told us not to—"

He shook his head, slowly and sadly. "Marty, Marty, still playing by the rules, huh? You can't take these things literally. She's a very cool lady. You'd like her. Want some advice?"

"No."

"I'm worried about Emily and Eleanor—they look tired. Don't work 'em so hard."

"Who asked you?"

His head was still now, and his eyes unwavering. "It doesn't matter what you do," he whispered, "you're gonna lose. Pardon my Uzbeki."

I was totally perplexed. Not by the Nemesis's weirdness—I didn't trust that at all. He was a weasel who'd mind-fuck a man till the condom fell off. No—the disturbing nugget was of course that he'd gone ahead and *called the client.* Against orders. What was I to do?

"Bartholomew," I said to my office mate, "I've got a problem."

"Can't help you."

It occurred to me that if it hadn't been for the incidents with the lighting and the speakerphone, he might have been willing to toss me a bone. But there was no bone.

My issue was that the client was herself going to pick a winner, and since the Nemesis had some kind of dialogue going with her he would have a much better idea of what she was looking for.

So I called the main client switchboard and asked for Sherry's office.

She answered on the first ring, and I introduced myself.

"Oh," she said, "you aren't working on the proposal, are you?"

"Yes, I am."

"I can't really talk about that. But how can I help you?"

"I understand you've been talking to one of my colleagues here."

Silence.

"Um," I said, "I'm wondering if you had any more information on what you're looking for."

"Who is this?" she asked, and I told her my name again. "Did you get the brief—the proposal request?"

"Yes," I said. "But is there more? Apparently you told my co-worker something about the approach—"

"It's in the brief."

"But—"

"Sorry, that's the other line. I'll see you."

And she hung up.

A few hours later, I went to the regular department meeting in the conference room on the 24th floor. The forty-odd members of our group sat around a huge oval table. My boss was halfway down, the Nemesis sat at the top, some of the new kids hung on counter space around the room's edge; I chose a seat against the wall near the door so I could leave if things got dull, or if my diet started talking back to me.

In my mind, my acting coach Al said: *Use this opportunity to assert yourself. Send a message about the New You.*

The agenda was mostly administrivia about an upcoming intra-office move we were making, new hires and exits, a little on financial results and key client updates.

Imaginary Al kept screaming in my ear: *Look at the Nemesis. He's got the power seat, right at the end. See, even if it's an oval table there's a power seat. Look how his shoulders are forward like he's about to tackle the speaker. See his comment right there didn't make any sense, he just said that to show he's here. Interrupt now, Marty. Do it!*

"That design sucks," I blurted, interrupting my boss walking us through a floorplan of the space we were moving to.

All eyes immediately turned to me—and I realized, with horror, that I had absolutely nothing to say. I'd committed myself now, of course. But of the world of possible things to get all Alpha about, I should probably not have chosen architecture. I have no visual sense at all. My idea of a well-designed room is one with a big dog in it.

"I'm sorry?" asked my boss. "Marty—you had a comment?"

I persisted: "All the offices are in the middle—and, and the cubes are around the sides. That means the VPs don't get any light."

"We talked about this—"

"It doesn't seem like you should get promoted *away* from a window."

"They're already built—"

"I'm just saying," I said, not sure what I was just saying, "that—you know. It's dark."

"You get light, Marty," she said, turning back to her floorplan walk-through.

"Any comments?" she said at the end. "Marty? Still too dark?"

People tittered, and invisible Al said: *What do you care? Someday you can fire them all, just to watch them cry.*

At that moment I suddenly understood a study I'd read recently. It said assertive behavior was more common in one-on-one situations than in larger groups and used more often against friends than enemies. The hypothesis was that groups tend to "water down" the threat, spread it over more victims, so that any given member of the group feels less personally at risk. Messing with a big group just feels silly.

During announcements the Nemesis said: "Yo, I wanted to remind you about my party Friday night. You're all invited, bring anyone you want, and B-Y-O if you're planning on getting yo'self hammered. Ha ha."

"What's the occasion?" someone asked.

"Nothing, just wanted to thank you all for great work."

"Are you going somewhere?" asked the boss, and people laughed, but not the boss herself.

Finally there was a call for volunteers to host the Kids' Room for Bring Your Kids to Work Day next week, and the Nemesis actually raised his hand. I smelled a rat.

"You're being all Mr. Team Spirit today," said the boss as she wrote the Nemesis's name down on the volunteer list.

"I love you guys," said the Nemesis.

Granted, it might have been my diet, but I suddenly felt like throwing up again.

I excused myself and went into the bathroom, hovering over the porcelain savior for a few minutes until the pain went away.

As I was washing my hands, the Nemesis came in and said, "You look like a turd on legs."

That night I quit the Warrior/Asshole Diet. And I have to say the hot fudge, butterscotch, Oreo, M&M, Aunt Jemima syrup and Froot Loops sundae I made for myself was about the yummiest three things I have ever had in my life.

STEP

NINE

Never Surrender

"Victory is gained by surprise."

—Sun Tzu,
The Art of War

Some sage once said pain is the touchstone of spiritual growth. Right now you're feeling a lot of that spiritual growth. The fantasies of tailored boxers and factory-installed seat warmers that kept you going in the early days have been beaten back by the reality of surly analysts, baffled family and friends, and poco-loco clients. In this Step, you learn self-doubt is optional.

You also learn that "Triumph" isn't just an incredible '80s Canadian power trio. It was also the battle cry for all the monumental jerks who came before us, the ancient Assholes who paused in their endless slaughter long enough to write the entire history of the world. And philosophy. And dating.

Now, I'd say my marriage was traditional in the sense that I did what my wife told me to do when she told me to do it. I'm sure there are other ways to stay married—more modern ways—but I don't know what they are. For some reason I decided to experiment with my winning formula that weekend at Fairway Market on the Upper West Side.

To enter this Manhattan version of a gourmet superstore is to realize quickly that the biggest pricks in the world are not Wall Street BSD's (Big Swinging Dicks)—they're old ladies with metal sticks and prostheses. It's like their whole life they've been in training to seize every advantage, jump on every sign of weakness in the aisles. They are absolute masters.

We walked into the produce section and immediately some old lady in yellow duck boots tried to start something with me. But she clearly didn't realize who I was.

"Do you mind?!" she snorted, grabbing for my basket. I'm not sure why she did this, but it may have had something to do with the fact that she had selected it first.

I pried it from her knotty hands—not an easy task.

"That's mine," I said.

"I was here first!"

"I'd like to see you prove it—"

"Gimme that!"

"Martin," my wife glared at me, getting in on the basket-pulling contest. Now we had three adults tussling over the thing, with a line of irate geriatrics rapidly piling up behind us. "Just give it to her—I'm sorry, ma'am—"

"Talk about rude—"

"Talkin' about yourself," I said, yanking the basket away from these two crazy women and stepping back.

"As if!—" The geezer grabbed another one, snorted something I shouldn't repeat, and trotted off throwing wicked looks behind her.

"What's wrong with you?" Gloria asked, handing me a sheet of paper.

"What's this for?" I shot back.

"It's the list."

"What do I do with it?"

"Go," she said patiently, "get that stuff. And don't get the wrong parsley like last time."

"How did I know there's two kinds of parsley?"

"Read the sign, Einstein."

There was something about her tone. It didn't agree with what I was thinking was the tone of the wife of a true Asshole. The wife wouldn't necessarily be a pushover, but she certainly wouldn't be like Gloria. All sarcastic and mouthy.

Now gurus and thinkers tend to say that we should not look at our failures as, well, "failures," but rather as opportunities to learn and improve. Let's say that what I decided to do next was a very good set of these learning-and-improvement opportunities.

Opportunity #1: I studied the list in my hand and decided to comment on it.

"What's this for? There's a lot of vegetables."

"It's *coq au vin*," said my wife. "I'll see you at the check—"

"What? Cock ow van? Why can't we have something else?" Too late I remembered Alpha Males never ask questions. "We're having something else."

She looked at me. "Okay," she said, "What?"

"Meatloaf."

"Sorry," she said, shaking her head.

"What's wrong with meatloaf?" Another question. I would really have to practice this more. "We're having it."

"So you're cooking?"

"No—I mean, you're the cook. You went to cooking school. I hate the way I cook—"

"Makes two of us. Now don't forget—flat parsley."

Then she went off to get the Ball & Evans chicken and nitrite-free bacon, and I was left to sift through all those identical gobs of wet green grass, kicking the geezers out of my line of sight the whole time.

Opportunity #2 happened at the checkout and was brought on when Gloria looked into the basket I was carrying. On my way, I'd dropped in some things that weren't on the list. Just a few things for me. Some packages of Brent & Sam's chocolate chip and raisin pecan cookies, and also some of those Sarabeth's pumpkin muffins that go so well with Ronnybrook Hudson Valley vanilla ice cream, which I'd also picked up.

"Oh, no," she said, pursing her lips, "put that back. Did you get the vegetables? I can't see—"

"They're in there." With all the transfats-and-sucrose products I'd piled on top of them, you couldn't see the real food.

"Put that stuff back."

"But," I whimpered, "it's organic."

"You don't need that. I thought you're trying to lose weight—"

"I can eat what I want."

"No. No you can't."

"Who says?"

"I say."

"You are not the boss of me."

"Yes I am. Now put that back."

The lines at Fairway are legendary for both their size and the aggression of their members. Now we were moving ahead but still quite far away from the registers, crammed against dozens of seniors and sad moms with Maclaren strollers, and it seemed like just about every one of them was listening to our little scene. In fact, the ninety-year-old behind us liked Gloria's "Yes I am" line so much he coughed out a laugh.

"Mind yourself," I said to him, and turned back to my wife. "I can eat what I want. You've got to stop bossing me."

"You need a boss."

"No I don't. Why do I need a boss?"

" 'Cause you're a big baby. Now put that back, line's moving."

"That's a mean thing to say."

"You can cry later—put that stuff—"

"Take it back."

"What?"

"What you said—take it back."

She shook her head, turned away from me and, miraculously, the line moved so we could actually get checked out. The Asshole had also checked out, apparently. He had met his match.

As my organic vanilla ice cream was melting on the subway ride home—reminding me why I never bought ice cream (too much time pressure)—I had mixed feelings. I had my baked goods in hand, but Gloria was buried in O magazine, which was never a good sign.

It was here on the No. 1 train around 103rd Street that I enjoyed Opportunity #3.

"You've got to stop treating me like a kid," I said.

"But you are one."

"See that's—I'm not one. I'm a man."

"A real man?"

"That's right. And I can do what I want."

"Look," said my wife, peering up finally from her *O* article on combating spousal abuse, "I can see you're trying to be all assertive lately. *Oooh ooh*"—like a gorilla—"and all. But don't try it at home."

"Why not? Don't you think our marriage can . . .?" here I trailed off, because I wasn't sure what I meant to say.

"Nothing's perfect, right? But those guys you're so in love with—all those macho men, there's a reason they're all on their third or fourth wives. Women don't like them. Not as husbands."

"I don't think that's true."

"I'll put it this way," she said, with a smile in her eyes. "You can treat me like shit—and I won't leave you. But you're gonna have to be making a hell of a lot more money."

Men are more evolved, I think. It doesn't matter to us how much money a woman has, unless she happens not to have big tits. And for an ass man like myself, they don't even have to be all that big.

Anyway, Gloria may have mussed up my mojo, but she definitely cleared things up for me. I had a new resolve in my mission. I was going to make more money, no matter who I had to jump on the street to do it.

I actually saw the woman sitting on the other side of my wife light up after she said the thing about making more money. Our eyes met, and she looked away. And as I got off the train at our stop, this guy I thought was buried in his PSP the whole way gave me a thumbs-up and said: "Go get her, tiger!"

Asshole.

Over the next few days I persisted in calling the client, Sherry, and she was progressively less and less polite. What kept me going was that study I mentioned about how aggressive salespeople may not be popular, but they make a lot more in commissions. I printed out the abstract and taped it to the wall behind my phone. Then I did what they call in the boiler-room world "smile 'n dial."

"Hi, Sherry, it's Marty again," I'd begin.

"Oh. So what can I do for you?"

"Just wondered if I could get your take on something?"

Without waiting for her to tell me she was running late for a meeting with the CFO, I launched into a quick scenario I'd preplanned for her. "Say we were to make a deal with manufacturers to use our influentials as a product testing lab, like for early versions and prototypes?"

"Sounds interesting. Like I said, you—"

"They'd feedback about these betas, maybe on an web-based tool."

"Put it in the pitch—"

They weren't long conversations, but I was practicing my own type of total aggression. I was not about to let the Nemesis monopolize client ear time unchallenged.

The Nemesis, meanwhile, continued in his suspicious sweet-guy ways, getting very active in Bring Your Kids to Work and even going so far as to host an *ice cream break* on our floor. He wore an apron and scooped the stuff himself. Complimented us on what a "special bunch of monkeys" we all were.

He seemed to be fooling the whole division. I heard people talk *sotto voce* about how he was "making an effort" and—heresy of heresies—"not so bad, really."

What, I wondered, does he have up his polyester sleeve?

I was about to find out.

• • •

One morning I was out walking Hola, and I saw my old antagonist Ramón getting pulled along by Misty. He made a point of taking her across the street to avoid running into us head on. That seemed like an overreaction, so I shouted: "Hey, Ray! Who's walking who over there?!"

He put down his phone long enough to say, "Take a hike!"

"That's exactly what I'm doing, fella!"

Ramón had been rude. Still—it was a pleasure to see that Hola was quantum leaps better behaved on the lead now than Misty, who was pulling her so-called master across Riverside Drive into traffic in a way that filled me with a feeling of déjà vu.

At Twin Donut, the mop guy had been replaced by a new woman with a superhuman sweet tooth. I think she believed the words "no sugar" meant "only two sugars," instead of the usual eight. In her world, nothing had no sugar. I thought she was a temporary sub for the mop fellow, but it turned out to be more permanent.

"What happened to the little guy?" I asked her.

"He get fired. How many sugar?"

"Fired? Why?"

"Somebody complain. Six sugar?"

It wasn't that I felt guilt over the small person's fate—it's possible his bionic lack of focus had been noticed by others, after all. It's just that I couldn't remember specifically aiding a service worker's unemployment before. I'd gone into new territory.

It felt kind of good.

• • •

The presentation that Friday was internal—for my boss, a few other account VPs, some of my peers, and the EVP. My team and the Nemesis's go head to head and the EVP, Gretchen, would decide which of our approaches to take to the competitive pitch at the client's on Monday.

The meeting was scheduled for eleven a.m. I got there thirty minutes early to make sure the projector was working and would talk to my laptop. More presentations are ruined by lighting and cables than by any human being.

It was at about ten to eleven that I started to wonder.

The Nemesis and I hadn't spoken in a while and had no co-ordinated timing. I was going to push for second, after the Nemesis, because one of my Alpha books had mentioned the last item on any agenda is the one that is most easily remembered.

But what happened was the Nemesis's team hadn't showed up. At five-to I called up to his office. Nobody answered.

People started straggling in—including Emily and Eleanor.

At five minutes after eleven, the EVP arrived with the Nemesis.

"Okay," she said, sitting down and looking at me. "What have you got?"

I wasn't sure what to do. "You can go—"

"It's alright," said the Nemesis, who'd had his head all but shaved and seemed very well rested and clean. Had I seen him in khakis before? "Age before beauty. Ha ha."

It took me a few minutes to get up a head of steam, but it went well. We'd done a lot of work, nothing but work lately. I'd driven the team like I was a guy who had balls of steel-plated iron with an all-weather coating.

It was when I arrived at the paid-referral argument the EVP challenged me.

"How open are we, do you think?" she asked. "Do we tell these kids we need a positive referral even if they hate the product?"

"Think about it," I said, "it's like any job, right? We do what we're paid to do even if we're lying. That's just life. I don't really see it as a problem."

"What about ethically?" asked the Nemesis, which was amazing coming from a prick like him. Maybe he heard about ethics on an episode of *The Apprentice*.

"I don't see a problem," I said. "Honestly. What is it?"

"Well," pushed the Nemesis, "maybe we should be encouraging kids to tell the truth. Just a thought."

There was an actual *tee-hee* from Emily.

"Keep going," said the EVP, so I did.

The Nemesis went after me, but his performance was a little muted. He took about half as long as I had, and his slides were patently the result of less work. It wasn't sloppy, just a bit underbaked.

Afterwards I tried to buttonhole him, but he slipped out when I was packing up the projector, and I had to wait till he got back from lunch. Jaime and Roger hadn't showed for the presentation, and it turned out they'd taken a long weekend together snowboarding at Hunter Mountain.

I was waiting in his office.

"Ah, nice job," he said. He'd been drinking wine, and I noticed his black leather belt looked brand new.

"How was lunch?" I asked.

"An SVP took me to Pastis. Awesome broiled salmon. Truly amazing."

"What's going on?" I asked him. "Lunch with senior managers—what's—what's going on?"

His phone rang. He winked at me while his eyeballs scanned his caller ID.

"That's Sherry—gotta take it—"

It was unbelievable but I had no other choice, so I left.

Next day the boss told me I'd won the face-off, and I said I kind of thought the Nemesis wasn't really trying and I was confused.

"What're you complaining about?" she asked me. "You get a chance to pitch to the client. This is a big deal."

"I guess. You're right."

I'd won.

It was not what I had dreamed, somehow. But whatever. One of the articles I'd read described a study of 134 managers at a utility plant. This study seemed to show that being assertive and self-centered did *not* necessarily lead to job satisfaction. In fact—incredible but true fact—the managers who were happiest in this particular survey were those who actually *cared about other people*. That is not a misprint. So Assholes acted as they did either out of bad habit or for reasons other than enjoyment on the job.

I stared at my phone, hoping even my crazy uncle would call. Nobody did, not even my friend Ben, who spent his life calling people. I was afraid of Gloria. I didn't want to stay and I didn't want to go home. My stomach felt like shit due to the lingering damage done by the Asshole Diet™, and I was hungry but afraid to eat. I couldn't even drink anymore.

If I'd had any feelings I'd have felt happy for myself. But the

Asshole turns all feeling into rage; that is his secret. I thought: *I'm getting weak.*

What I needed was encouragement. So I took out a pad of paper with the client's logo on it and I made a list headed "Great Asshole Institutions." It included such notorious viper dens as McKinsey & Co., the Navy SEALs, Goldman Sachs, the Walt Disney Company, and the Catholic Church.

What a crew!

Wasn't it true, after all, that the greatest institutions in the world were populated by A-1 Assholes? This was indisputable. Did they worry if they spent some time alone after a meeting, wishing for a friend or a kind word, waiting for a murmur of fellowship that would never, ever come?

Of course not. The idea was laughable. They were too busy ruling the world.

This made me feel better. Another activity that improved my resolve was a couple hours' historical research. *Research?!* you ask. *I can barely understand this sentence I'm reading right now! How can I do research!?*

Don't worry—I did it for you. From various sources, including my own vague memories from high school, I pieced together a brief time line of the world from prehistory to the present. And guess what I found out?

The world has always been owned and operated by a bunch of total Assholes, who were defeated by even bigger dickheads and schmuckleberries, and so on, until we end up with *Survivor: Marquesas.*

Here's what I mean:

THE ASSHOLE'S HISTORY OF THE WORLD

B.C.

1.6 million	Fire invented. Many years later, used to attack defenseless marshmallows.
10,000	Humans domesticate plants and animals—commence destruction of every living thing.
900	Aptly named ASSyrians of northern Mesopotamia begin conquering nearby, sweeter tribes.
550	Confucius and Buddha develop their philosophies, which have kept non-Assholes serenely confused for centuries.
327	Alexander the Great celebrates his marriage to Roxana, daughter of Oxyartes, by invading India and, later, Roxana's pants.

A.D.

30	Jesus, possible Son of God and really nice guy, is killed.
1100	Feudal system adopted throughout Europe, leading to numerous feuds, which they really should have seen coming.
1206–27	Reign of Genghis Khan, legendary Mongol fucktard.
1291	The final Crusade ends. Victory party is muted because most of the participants are dead or getting the shit tortured out of them.
1513	Machiavelli's *The Prince* published.
1900's	World Wars I and II, Korea, Vietnam, Iraq, et cetera point to world not getting nicer anytime soon.
1989	Berlin Wall falls. United Germany wins title of Biggest Asshole Nation, unseating momentarily mellower U$A.
2000	*Survivor* debuts.
2008	*A$$hole* erupts.

All this musing on history got me wondering if there was anything I could learn from great thinkers of the past. The philosophers of Assholism. Who were they, anyway? Turns out there are four.

The first was the legendary Sun Tzu, author of the classic *The Art of War*. This practical guide to dickdom has been studied and handed down through generations of Hollywood talent agents since the late 1980's. Master Sun's observations have a timeless quality that is as true today as when he wrote them more than twenty centuries ago:

- "One with great skill appears inept"
- "If you take on too much . . . you will eventually be drained"
- "In a chariot battle, reward the first to capture at least ten chariots"

The next great Asshole philosopher was, of course, Niccolò Machiavelli, author of that flawless guide to office politics, *The Prince*. Machiavelli, writing in the early 1500's, understood that people are fundamentally "ungrateful, fickle, pretenders and dissemblers, evaders of danger, eager for gain." And those are the good things.

As he said:

- "It is much safer to be feared than loved"
- "Always be out hunting"

The next great jerk-thought-leader was the German Friedrich Nietzsche, who was a lifelong atheist, which accounted for his limp. Nietzsche felt we should all aspire to be "supermen" who are "beyond good and evil." And he summed up his vision for humanity with the inspiring words: "Entertain the hope that life may one day become more evil and more full of suffering than it has ever been."

It was hard for me to believe this power trio of Sun Tzu, Machiavelli, and Nietzsche could be improved upon as the intellectual rock stars of my new life, but—amazingly—it could. The greatest of Asshole philosophers turned out to be a woman whose name I'd first heard mentioned in reverent whispers by members of the Math Club back in high school. And, more recently, by the Nemesis.

That sacred name was Ayn Rand.

What did Rand believe? In *The Virtue of Selfishness* she said people should never accept "unearned guilt" by realizing that "man must live for his own sake" and not "sacrific[e] himself to others." And she totally hated losers (like, say, the Dalai Lama) who "advise [man] to turn himself into a totally selfless 'schmoo' that seeks to be eaten by others."

A horrible thought occurred to me—that I was just such a "schmoo"—and I didn't even know what one was. It was sad being a schmoo. It was lonely in schmoo-land. People danced all over me singing their happy songs—why?—because I was, at the end of the day, just fundamentally a *schmoo* . . . probably with some vague "altruistic motives."

Ick.

If you've followed my plan faithfully you'll be experiencing mood swings right now. They won't make sense, then they will, then they won't. It's like you're spinning faster around your own life, but getting closer and closer to the center. If you're like me you'll feel sick, angry, nauseous, exhilarated, and scared—and that's just before breakfast.

Maybe it was the sobering march through history, or that glimpse at Ayn Rand. Maybe it was the hollow sound ringing in my head since I'd "won" my confrontation with the Nemesis. Maybe I was just lonely.

Whatever the reason, there was enough pinging across my face to alarm Gloria that weekend, as we were standing in our neighborhood dog park, closely watching Hola as she nose-tackled the local pit-bulls and Rottweilers.

"Let me guess," she said, leaning back against the fence, "it didn't go well."

"What?" I really didn't know what she was talking about.

"The face-off with the Nemesis. You lost, right? It's okay."

What I couldn't believe was I had forgotten to tell her what had happened. What was wrong with me?

"No," I said, "we won."

She whipped her eyes away from Hola to me, not doing much to hide her surprise. "You beat him?"

"Yup."

"That's weird."

"Thanks a lot."

"Was he sick or something?"

"It's like he didn't even try," I said, luring Hola away from a couple of troublemakers with a shred of Gouda.

"Well," she said after a moment, "maybe you're just better."

"I don't know," I shook my head. "I've seen him more on fire. He didn't work the team that hard. Let them go early most nights. He's acting kind of weird—like he's a nice guy."

"Like you used to be."

"Right, like I—"

I let Hola go and faced Gloria. *Like you used to be.* That hurt. But it didn't make me mad, exactly; it was true. Her wife-dar was working.

"I'm sorry," I said, meaning it. "I guess I—"

"Hey," she said, "it's probably just stress. You know, you beat the Nemesis. Think about that! That's amazing."

"Yeah," I admitted. "it's pretty coolio."

"Super-coolio," she said. "And Hola's doing better, you're not walking that crazy Misty. Right? You look good for that promotion. Sweet money. Am I wrong? Life is not bad."

Everything she said was right. What was I all mopey about? I started to forget.

"Yeah," I admitted. "Life is good."

"Now go rescue your girl." She pointed over to where Hola was being scouted by a very small, very horny mini-pinscher. Like me, he was having a hard time getting up the courage to finish off his evil plan.

S T E P

Life Is a Gift, So Return It

T E N

This final Step is a taking stock of your journey and a charting of the road forward. Like the weary travelers at the end of *The Wizard of Oz*, you discover that your destination is not quite what you had imagined. To be an Asshole seemed a glorious thing. And it is. Sort of. Painful as it is, the message here is one of self-acceptance. Even if you're—ugh—you.

I skipped the Nemesis's house party, which was about as rude as his neglecting to invite me in the first place. Which brings us to the Lucifer pitch.

Emily and Eleanor had decided on the passive approach to office work; that is, they'd answer me when I spoke to them but offer nothing on their own. They looked terrible, despite being dressed up for a meeting with the EVP. I chose not to care. I should have seen it coming: I'd read in the *International Journal of Organization Theory and Behavior* that the most common reaction to a jerk in the workplace is "avoidance."

"Did you make the copies?" I asked.

"Yes," said Eleanor.

"Twelve of them?"

"Fifteen."

"Color?"

"Only green and white, like you asked—"

"*What—?!!*"

"Marty, I'm kidding. They're color."

"Where are they?"

"On your desk."

"Is there a projector?"

And so on. It was clear—if I had been into parsing situations and moods the way the old Marty had—that they'd come to some kind of understanding between them, based upon the weeks just past. So I wasn't surprised when, as I was leaving the team room, Eleanor said, "Can I talk to you a second?"

"I need to—"

"I'll walk with you."

Which is what she did, saying, with some nervousness, "When is this project over, do you think?"

"Depends on what the client says."

"Emily and I would like—we'd like to go on a different engagement. Next week."

I stopped and looked at her.

"We don't want to do this one anymore," she said.

"Well that's not up to you, is it?"

"I guess—"

"See you downstairs, okay?"

The pitch itself was at the client's tower on Long Island. I went to the bathroom and double-checked my face didn't have anything funny on it before we headed down to the limo on Eighth Avenue.

My team seemed a smidge nervous, which made sense when I found out what Emily planned to lay on me on the way down.

She'd maneuvered her way onto the back seat between me and Eleanor, who spent most of the ride poking her BlackBerry with her thumbnails.

As we turned onto the FDR and headed north, Emily said:

"I don't wanna bother you but some of us . . . have been . . . Let me start over. It just seems like you've been upset a little lately and . . . Are you?"

"What?"

"You've been acting weird," said Eleanor, not looking up from her device.

"Yeah," said Emily, "and it's—it seems like you're upset at us. Are you—are you mad at me?"

"Should I be?"

"Then what's going on? Do you not want to—not want to talk about it? 'Cause that's cool—"

"There's nothing to talk about."

"Okay, then."

"Let's worry about ourselves," I said.

"Fine."

"*Can you go any slower?!*" I shouted over the seat at the driver, who flipped me the finger with his eyes in the rearview.

We were early, so I had time to ensure the projector worked. It was in a nice executive meeting room on the 50th floor.

Weather held sweet and clear and the smog glowed blue like a screensaver.

About five minutes later my boss came in with the EVP. Four of the client people who'd been in the meeting last month where I'd impressed Gretchen—the one where I first stood up to the Nemesis—also came in and took spots around the large oval table. My boss grabbed a couple waters and asked if the Nemesis was coming.

"He didn't ride with you?" I asked.

"Nope."

"Then I don't know." My paranoia radar beeped: What kind of a game was he playing here anyway?

Sherry came in. She was a pleasant looking, rather suburban-type woman with a monogrammed pullover and hairsprayed blond hair. Her greeting was polite if not warm, and she ignored her colleagues.

"Okay," she said, poking open a Sprite Zero tab with a clear-lacquered nail, "let's start."

The Nemesis wasn't there—and, to save you any suspense, I'll reveal he didn't show up. Later I found out he'd called Gretchen in the car to say he couldn't make it, but for now I was just confused. I dove in.

Standing to the side of the screen holding the Sharp remote slide-changer, I went through the material I'd rehearsed. It took about thirty-five minutes, with twenty at the end for discussion, so we ended more or less on time.

"How do we find these influentials?" asked one of the client team, a ferret-like guy with a shiny nose.

"Two ways," I said. "We can use algorithms to track online behavior and build look-alike models to profile likely targets.

These are based on a sample of knowns correlated to behavior. The track modeling pops out best-fit analogues and we can calibrate as we test-and-learn down the line."

Since nobody in the room had any idea what I meant by this—including me—the guy asked, "What's the other way?"

"We ask them."

"We just say, 'Hey, are you influential?' "

"There's ways to do it better than that. We can ask people in their networks to   "

"What about the payments?" interrupted Sherry. "I don't know that a paid referral model works. Haven't we s—"

"Hold on," I interrupted. "What's your data point?"

Gretchen and my boss were looking uncomfortable. They made some vague noises, but I said, "Huhn?"

"I don't have—"

"Look," I said, "this isn't altruism here. We're like Ayn Rand. Somebody does something for us, we pay them. If the kids don't feel they can—*recommend* the product, why should they benefit? What's in it for us?"

"Who's Ayn Rand?" somebody asked.

It was around then that my cell phone chose to ring: *"Pick up the phone, playa! This is Ice-T! Pick up the phone!!"*

Someone said, "Wow."

We had a few more back-and-forths and Sherry stood and said, "Thanks, guys, that was great," and left the room, rapidly followed by her duckling-like colleagues.

I had Eleanor dismantle the projector and Emily gather the leftover copies as I went to where my boss and Gretchen were whispering.

"What'd you think?"

"Nice ring tone," said my boss.

"Oh my God," said Gretchen, "look how late—I've got another—"

And how did I feel? Remember that I'd done dozens of pitches in the past and will no doubt do many more in the future. And all I really know is that you never know. Sometimes they're wizardly and you wait months to not get the call; other times, you stumble through a bunch of shit and end up with a big whopping bag of loot.

You never know.

I was doped with fatigue when I got into work the next morning.

"Gretchen was looking for you," said my office-mate as I punched my code into the phone.

There were four messages. One from my boxing coach Carlos, telling me not to get all flabby (too late). Two from my boss, telling me to call her when I got in. And one from Gretchen, saying, "Come see me when you get this."

I'd never been summoned to the EVP's office first thing like that before. Also, she'd never come looking for me personally, as Bartholomew seemed to be saying. I was definitely moving up in the world.

Although very tired as I climbed the round staircase to the floor above, where Gretchen's office was, I felt better. My insides were healing and I knew the worst was past. I was even wondering what kind of a car I could get with my huge bonus.

I loved life, and it loved me.

Until I opened the door to Gretchen's office, saw my boss sitting on the little designer couch, caught the EVP herself scowling at the yellow cabs down on Eighth Avenue, and the red light on the speaker phone indicating a caller.

Gretchen swung around as I came in and said, "Amit, we'll call you back. Marty just walked in."

"Okay," said Amit, who was the head of our Saskatchewan operation, and rang off.

"So," said Gretchen, "how're you feeling?"

"Okay."

"Have a seat. Got a message from Sherry this morning to call her, so there's probably some news. Let's do it"—she opened the door and screamed out for her assistant, Ambrose, to get Sherry on the speaker, which Ambrose rapidly did.

Then Gretchen closed the door and we hovered around the phone, talking to the disembodied voice.

Sherry was the one with the budget. And I could tell from her "Hello, guys" she wasn't going to make my day. My Mercedes CLS550 evaporated.

"I just want to thank you guys for coming in to pitch," said Sherry. "I know it was late notice, and you did a great job considering."

That *considering* stung.

"But," she continued, "we're gonna go with someone else. A smaller agency. We liked your approach, but it just didn't seem like where we wanted to go right now. So thanks again so much. We appreciate the work you put into it. Thanks."

If she thanked us again for failing her I was going to emote.

"Okay, of course," said Gretchen, who'd been through this a million times in her career, "we respect that. Do you have any feedback for us? On the pitch, or the team, whatever? So that next time—"

"Well, I wasn't gonna bring this up," said Sherry, so quietly

Gretchen had to ramp up the volume on the phone, "but since you asked. Is Marty there?"

"I'm here," I said.

"Marty, we haven't worked together before," she said. "And I thought you were very prepared. But I just wasn't comfortable with your reaching out to me before the proposal."

Both my boss and Gretchen looked at me with new eyes.

"I was pretty clear about not talking to any of the teams involved, and I didn't appreciate that you, you know, broke the silence. No big deal, really. But it just gave me a sense it would be harder to work with you."

"But," I said, "I wasn't the only one who reached out—"

"I'm sorry," said Sherry, "yes, you were. And I thought it was aggressive."

"But—"

"That shouldn't have happened," said Gretchen, "and we're sorry. Just some confusion on our part. Next time we'll be more buttoned up. I am sorry."

"No big deal. Really. Gotta run—"

She hung up, and it hit me what had happened. There was no way around it. This was the kind of fiendish, dare I say Machiavellian, maneuver I thought only happened in fiction or down on Wall Street. The Nemesis had set me up, lied to me, got me to call the client, and crippled my career.

I had been out-Assholed by the Ass-Master himself.

Surprisingly, it was the EVP who gave me the benefit of the doubt, not my boss. She'd seen me deteriorating for weeks now. Gretchen still thought of me, I suppose, as nice Marty.

"What happened?" she asked me.

"[The Nemesis] told me she was okay with calling, so I called her, once or—"

"Don't put this on him," said my boss.

"But he—"

"Just. Don't. You heard her say he didn't call her—"

"So he lied to me."

"That's hard to believe," said my boss.

"But it's true—!"

"Guys, guys," interjected the EVP, "it's over. Win some, lose some, right? Let's move on. And you"—she looked directly at me, in my stare-off zone in a triangle on my forehead—"need to learn from this. That's all. Now, I've got a nine-thirty—"

I took advantage of the fact that everybody hated me now to have a nice quiet lunch by myself on Eighth Avenue. It gave me some time to think. When I couldn't come up with any happy thoughts at all, I called my friend Brad and left a another message. He owed me like five calls. Then I tried my friend Ben and also got voicemail.

I could not remember a time in the twelve years I'd known him that Ben had failed to pick up his phone. The guy barely had a job, for God's sake. He did absolutely nothing all day but answer his phone and talk to his friends.

Just then, a group of my co-workers walked down Eighth Avenue directly in front of the window of the diner—some of the same co-workers who'd told me not fifteen minutes earlier they were "not going out for lunch today."

Hmmm.

I would have called my wife—who knows, she might even have picked up—but I didn't want to lose all my faith in people.

So I finished up my cold, stale Belgian waffle and overpaid

for it. I tried to say something nice to the cashier, but she glared at me in two languages.

Tomorrow's another day, I was thinking hopefully as I neared the big revolving doors letting into the agency's lobby and saw about the last person I ever expected to see being escorted out of the building by a security person.

Yes—it was the Nemesis. Out on the street.

Holding a box and looking triumphant.

He didn't notice me and quickly found a cab and got into it with his box. I watched the yellow cab pull into traffic and I made my way upstairs in the elevator and out onto my floor.

All the kids were atwitter, congregating around the Nemesis's office, which was empty. Most of the stuff had been swept off the top of his desk, but the poster of the ATM remained. Evidently he'd taken the blown-up credit card portrait with him.

"What happened?" I asked Emily.

"Well, all I saw was he came in, the door was closed—"

"What door?"

"The door to his office. He closed it and there was, like, screaming—"

"Wait, who? Who screamed?"

"Would you let me—so, he was in there on the phone, like, screaming at somebody. Or talking loud let's say. And then the security guys come—"

"How long after?"

"I don't know. Two minutes. He had the door open and he knew they were coming. He said, 'Wait a second, guys,' and they—they waited outside the door while he packed up the box.

Took like a minute. And then he's all walking down with one of them."

"You said there were two—"

"One went to the bathroom, duh," she said. "One of them, like, took him down."

Eleanor had wandered up behind me; I turned because I could smell something sweet. She was shaking her head.

"So," she said, "you got your wish, huh?"

"What?"

"He's gone."

"Where's he going?"

"Starting up his own agency—already had a big client, so he said."

Emily piped up: "He tried to get us to go with him."

"He did?!"

"Hit on a bunch of us. Quietly. Last week."

"Yeah," said Eleanor, "that's why he was being all nice and stuff recently. Weirdness."

"Why didn't you go with him?" I asked.

She seemed surprised by the question. "Think we're stupid?"

"Yeah," said Emily, "that guy's a jerk."

A couple other people I asked didn't have any more details, and the more senior people weren't in their offices, so I was left to wander up to Gretchen's office and ask Ambrose if he'd heard the news.

"Oh, yes," he sniffed, going through e-mail. I couldn't tell if he was talking to me or his headset.

"What happened?"

"Dunno."

"How'd you hear?"

"Only—he called Gretchen and—oh, sorry, Marty, I've gotta take this—"

I waited but he suddenly had a million things going on, and the EVP wasn't at her desk, so I had nothing to do but, reluctantly, go back to work.

On a hunch I called some people at the client's building to find out where they'd gone with Lucifer, but nobody knew yet, and I left a couple messages following up on leads for other work. My inbox was empty, my to-do checklist fully checked. I made an appointment for a hydrotherapy session at Aveda, then cancelled it because it seemed too indulgent. I spent a few hours doing nothing in particular on the Internet, with the sound turned off. I had nothing to work on.

Maybe, I mused, I could locate a person to berate, belittle, and betray, but I had so little energy because of that stupid diet. It was exhausting being a full-time Asshole. And it hurt me to sit: I had actually developed a case of hemorrhoids, the most shameful of—

"D'you have a second?"

My boss, in the doorway, arched her wrist to indicate I should follow her into her office, and a moment later we were settled and the door was closed.

She wasted no time, saying:

"You heard about [the Nemesis], right? He quit today."

"What happened?"

If I had to describe my boss' demeanor in this scene it would be startled. The angles of her face were flatter as though she'd been slapped, and she looked redder. She breathed audibly through her nose, and a half-empty Mountain Dew Slurpee from 7-11 squatted on the desk. Considering she was a woman so respectful of her temple she refused to consume any food that hadn't been taken from the ground by registered Democrats, I'd have to say that Slurpee was a cry for help.

Outside it was getting darker.

"Security took him out," said my boss, "around lunch."

"I know, I saw it."

"It's pretty bad." She waited a moment. "He—he's going out on his own."

"I heard," I said. "Like consulting? For who?"

"No—he's starting a full-service agency."

"In direct marketing?"

She nodded.

"But why the security? Did he do something?"

"No—it's policy, firm policy when somebody quits for a direct competitor they have to leave right away. Or in this case they go to start a competitor."

"Why's that?"

"I guess it's so they don't steal their contacts or any I.P."— Intellectual Property, presentations and spreadsheets.

"Who was he fighting with on the phone? How'd he quit?" I asked, remembering what Emily had told me she'd overheard.

"That was Gretchen. Probably when he told her. It's just— it's like the worst-case scenario, what he did."

"But why?" I asked, puzzled by her distress. "People quit all the time."

"It's the way he did it."

" 'Cause he went over your head to Gretchen? She's the Exec—"

"No," she said, getting sadder and sadder by the moment. As I said, her mood made no sense to me. I was getting quite a lift from this, personally. "You don't understand."

"What'd he do?"

My boss looked right at me and said:

"Remember we were talking to Sherry about Lucifer and she said she was going with a smaller agency?"

"Uh huh."

"Well—that smaller agency is—it's him basically. He took Lucifer and left."

"She's hiring him to consult?" I asked. I think the aftereffects of the Asshole Diet™ were slowing down my synapses.

"No," said my boss, *"she's giving him the whole project."*

"Wow."

It was amazing. That a relatively junior, unpopular VP at a middle-of-the-road agency won a multi-million dollar account contested by the best and brightest in the space—amazing. Again, the Ass-Master had earned his ranking.

This information explained why the Nemesis dropped out of our own pitch. It explained why he sabotaged me—extra insurance for his own triumph. It even explained why he was so nice to people near the end: He was looking for start-up employees.

It took my breath away.

What a first-class Asshole.

"It's gonna mean some retrenchment around here," said my boss. "He was one of our more *productive* VPs. We'll probably take a revenue hit. Jaime and Roger went with him. So there's implications on staffing and so on. Oh, and there's one other thing."

I was thinking she was going to lecture me again on how I'd

have to step up to the plate and *sell sell sell!* But I was wrong, as usual.

"Congratulations," she said to me.

"What?"

"You're promoted."

She wasn't really smiling, but I said, "Is that sarcastic?"

"No, Marty. You got the promotion. Go get 'em."

"So you're serious?"

"Completely."

"Okay—"

"I'll let you know the comp in a couple days. But we're gonna hold the bonus back."

"What's that mean?"

"Basically we're gonna hold it back contingent on the feedback."

"What?"

She swallowed. "Let's talk Friday."

"Let's talk now," I insisted.

She looked at the door to double-check it was closed, then she lowered her voice for extra insurance.

She said: "In your assessment there's some issues in which we need to see improvement."

"What issues?"

"Some of the junior people—it seems weird to be saying this, Marty—but some of the juniors don't like working for you. They say you're unfair."

"How? Who was it? Was it Emily?"

"Can't tell you that. You'll get all the—details—in the readout. The main point is we need to see improvement in your interpersonals before we can approve the bonus. Okay?"

"Interpersonals? Like what?"

"We need you to be *nicer*. Okay?"

I did not see that coming. Of all the things to say to me—
Be nicer?! What was she trying to do, make me insane?

"You have got to be kidding with me," I said, evenly.

Her cell phone rang. She seemed very relieved.

"No. I'm not. Now let me take this call—"

That Friday night I still didn't know what to do. My wife was
working at the school, my friend Ben had e-mailed he was in
Maine visiting his sick aunt, and Brad continued not to call me
back.

If you follow my program, you'll find that one advantage
of not having any friends left and being in a kind of Mexican
standoff with your job is that you have a whole lot of free time.
I could have spent this time watching TV, of course, except that
would mean I'd actually have to turn on the TV set. Every time
I did that, I felt like assassinating the entire U.S. Senate.

So TV was out. I did something I used to do a lot—wandered around Times Square imagining I was a tourist. It always
cheered me up. Visitors from out of town are a lot like my dog:
They're so happy to be where they are. Life is good! Boy am I
hungry! Can I have that pretzel?!

And there's so much electricity in Times Square. I don't
mean metaphorical, social electricity, I mean actual electricity.
I've heard the intersection of 44th Street and Broadway is visible
from outer space, like a welcome mat for aliens. That would ex-
plain what some of these people were wearing.

It occurred to me there may be a new Bruce Springsteen al-
bum out. Given that the last one I bought was about fifteen

years ago, this was a safe bet. So I went into the Virgin Megastore, strolled over to the rack of "S" CDs—and ran right into my friend Ben.

Awkward.

He looked totally shocked to see me—and his face flushed.

"How was Maine?" I asked him. "Is your aunt better already?"

"What? Oh, right. Maine."

We stood there a moment, both of us wondering who was going to die first.

More or less simultaneously, I said "You didn't go, did you?" and he said, "I didn't go."

Spontaneously saying the same thing at the same time as somebody else is always pretty funny, and it broke the ice.

"Good to see you, brother," he said. Then I went to hug him, and he hugged me back. Only we did this the way straight men do it, which is without actually hugging one another. It's more like a slight lean in the right general direction.

We stepped back, and I immediately started combing my hair.

"So what're you doing here?" I ask him.

"Nothing. You?"

"Same thing."

"Cool."

Pause. Comb. He watched a talented young lady walk by.

"Fuck it," said Ben, "let's see a movie."

So we did. And it was incredible, a truly moving combination of surgical instruments, heavy-duty power tools, limbs ripped off bodies, a guy in a leather mask, and hot chicks from Estonia. We gave it four thumbs up and two sequels.

Afterward we stopped by Carmine's to gain some pasta

weight. It was during this meal, after Ben's second glass of wine had arrived, that I took the risk of asking him if he was miffed at me.

"Hmmm," he said sheepishly. "I guess."

"Okay. Why?"

"You missed my reading, man."

"What reading? What're you talking about?"

"See—that's what I mean. You totally missed it."

Turns out a couple weeks earlier he'd done a staged reading of a play he'd written. If I was more spiritually evolved, I would have admitted—as I suddenly realized—I did get the invitation. I was just too deep into my mission at the time to care.

"I'm sorry," I said. "I didn't know about it. I've had a lot going on."

He nodded while I buttered my third roll.

"How's the asshole thing going?" he asked me.

"Sucky."

"Oh, really," he said, " 'cause I kind of think it's working."

All my many therapists have failed to cure me, obviously. But I'd had one who was better than the rest. For one thing, he didn't happen to think there was anything much wrong with me a little maturity wouldn't cure. For another, he was practical.

One of the techniques he taught me was called "self-counseling." During times of stress or confusion, he suggested, try writing a letter asking yourself for advice, and then try *answering* that letter. I recommend this to you. It really works. Sometimes.

Being out of better ideas, I gave his technique a whirl the

next day when I got to the office. My letter, and my response, went like this:

Dear Marty,

Considering how unhelpful you've been to me so far I hesitate to give this a chance. But due to a recent personality change, I don't seem to have many friends left to turn to. So here's my question:

What does it all mean?

I know that's a deep one, but I've come face to face with it and I feel like I'm not getting it yet.

A few months ago, after a performance review at work, I had a Eureka moment. I thought I'd figured out the thing that had been holding me back all my life. At that point I really believed that I was too much of a pushover and that if only I could make myself more dick-like all my problems would be solved. I'd make more money, dress better, have more sex—be more like the people I thought I wanted to be like.

But it didn't seem to work like I thought it would. Sure, I got promoted, but only because my rival for the position decided to quit. And I was aggressive with a client—totally out of character for me—but instead of respecting me for it, she hated it. And the people who used to like working for me have bailed, so I'm left either forcing people to do stuff or breaking in the new recruits who are lame.

My biggest problem is, I just don't know how to act anymore. Who am I? What are my instincts? Are they right or wrong? Do nice guys finish last? And if that's true, does it necessarily follow that not-nice guys finish first?

Can you help me?

Dear Marty,

Your questions touched me deeply and filled me with a kind of swelling joy. That is because you mentioned "a final chance"—which means if I let you down again, as I fully intend to do, then I won't have to answer any more of these ridiculous notes.

But moving on, the issues you raise are important. They touch on the nature of a life well lived, internal ethics, and who we are within the fabric of our communities, ourselves and our relation to the soul. So my first point is: Congratulations! You're not as shallow as you used to be.

As for an answer, I'm not sure I have one. Perhaps a few observations will suffice.

For instance: When are you going to *shut the fuck up!*?

You are a miserable pain in my ass. Do you really think you're the first person who wondered who they were, or what they should do with their lives? That's right: *Not!* You think you're a pushover and it's getting in the way of your success. Then here's a major brainwave for you, Tesla: *Stop being such a fucking pushover!* Make sense?

Didn't think so—that's because you are the worst case I've ever seen of a person who can't find his own dick with two hands and a map! Don't know how to act? How about this: *Act like you know.*

Anything you want that other people also want is going to take a lot of focus, effort and determination. Focus. Effort. Determination. Even then there's no guarantee, especially for people like you who have no natural talent for anything.

Now where—you're asking—are Marty's personal favorite ingredients of *whining, self-pity,* and *mental hypochondria?*

That's right, they're back where they belong: Shoved up your *ass!*

Does that help?

I printed out this letter to and from myself and read it over a couple times. Really thought about it. Then I tore it in half and put it into the blue recycling bin next to the vending machines. It was in that moment I finally knew what to do.

EPILOGUE

Doing What It Takes

"It is a disgrace to be rich and honored in an unjust state."

—Confucius

You were promised a path from Zero to Hero—and you got it! Riches and happiness are yours for the taking! Enjoy! True, the riches might not be in the form of actual money, at least not right away, and the joy might not be all hookers and blow . . . but by following the Ten Steps of Assholism you can gain something I didn't think you'd ever have: a soul.

At this point, as you can see, I had precious few options. I was backed into a corner, at a spiritual and physical crossroads. There was no way I wanted to do what I had to do next, but the Fates had left me no alternative. I had to call in the big gun.

I phoned my wife and begged her to meet me for lunch.

She was in the middle of class—as it turned out, the

ominously titled "Knife Skills." But something about the tone of my voice told her this meeting was probably included in the "worse" part of "for better or worse."

So she said she had "literally twenty minutes" and met me at Kosmo's on Eighth Avenue wearing a white canvas jacket with the name of her cooking school embroidered on an arm patch. First thing she did was insult the menu, then she told me how she'd rewrite it, then she described all the injuries her fellow students were getting in "Knife Skills." I actually counted to make sure she had all ten fingers.

Then she drank some water and asked me, "What's wrong, chief?"

"Gloria, I've got to tell you something."

She breathed in sharply. These are definitely not the words you want to be hearing from your spouse.

"Okay," she said, gingerly.

And I told her—about the decision to be an Asshole, the coaches and the field trips with Al ("You did *what?*" she asked when I told her about the hotdog cart); about practicing in stores and on my team at work; about the weird diet.

At some point the waiter came, and Gloria ordered a scotch and soda. He reminded her that Kosmo's was a diner, not a saloon.

After I finished, she just stared at me. I didn't know what to expect. This was basically a confession that I'd been lying to her for a couple of months. If she had decided to slap me, I would not have disapproved.

But she did something different: she breathed out suddenly, grabbing onto the table. Nodding slightly, she said, "Well, that's a relief. I thought you were having an affair."

"What?"

"With that girl Emily—the ballet dancer. You're always talking about her."

I couldn't believe this; it had never occurred to me she might think such a thing. But it made sense: I had been away and "working late" a lot lately, to accommodate my various experiments. I laughed, then almost cried, then laughed again. "She's not my type," I said.

"I knew you were up to something," she said, thinking back. "You've been kind of a jerk. But Hola's a lot better." She was nodding. "Yes, Hola's definitely shaped up. So have you, sort of. You look better."

"Thank you." I waited a moment. "Gloria, I'm sorry—"

"Don't be sorry," she stopped me. "That's the old Marty. You wanted to change, you made an effort. That's all that matters."

I worked on my chocolate pie and Gloria drank more water. She seemed anxious, like maybe she'd left something on the stove back at school. "So what's wrong?" she asked. "You seem upset."

I admitted, "Being an asshole isn't as great as I thought it would be."

She had to smile. "What were you expecting?"

"I don't know—something else."

"Come on," she said, gently. "You know what you expected. Tell me."

I thought back to the tan guy in the dog park, at the beginning of my journey. I said: "I guess I figured I'd just stop being nice and I'd get a better apartment. You know, love and respect. All that."

She looked like she might giggle. "Why'd you think that?"

"It seemed obvious."

I pondered for a moment. Then I said:

"I have a question."

"Okay."

"Why—why do I feel so bad about things? I'm not happy, Gloria."

She looked at her watch, then back at me. "I know why," she said.

"So tell me."

"You don't want me to."

I knew she was right. Of course she was right—she knew me better than anybody, even my dog. The only mystery being why she insisted on staying married to me.

"Go ahead," I said, "tell me. Don't worry about my feelings."

"You're not being who you are. It's like Aristotle said: 'To thine own self be true.' Life seems to work better that way."

"That wasn't Aristotle."

"Told you you didn't want to hear it."

She stood up and started rebuttoning her lab coat. There were pudding stains on it. Looked like yummy pudding. God, I loved pudding.

Suddenly, from nowhere, I let out a yawp of emotion I'd kept inside me all these months: *"I just want you to love me!"*

Talk about a conversation stopper. I know I got the complete attention of Kosmo's Diner.

After a moment, Gloria leaned down and kissed me. Then she stood up again, hovering.

"I do love you," she said, smoothly. "Whoever you are."

"Really? But why?"

"Lots of reasons."

"Give me one."

She considered this a moment. Then she said: "I think it's cute how you're always trying to improve yourself. It's adorable. A total waste of time—but it's adorable."

With another quick kiss, she left for the kitchen, having just served me up some food for thought.

If you've followed my Steps and done everything right—which is to say, wrong—you too will have your Moment of Truth. Probably in a diner, and probably with your S.O. It's not pleasant, but like any diagnosis it's better to know.

When you and I met, we thought we'd figured out the thing that had been holding us back all our lives. At that point we really believed we were too much of a pushover and that if only we could make ourselves more dick-like all our problems would be solved. We'd pull in more money, dress better, maybe get invited to Uma Thurman's Cool People Christmas Party, if she has one—be more like all the people we thought we wanted to be like.

But at least for me, it didn't work like that. I had to face the unexpected conclusion that being an Asshole all the time doesn't seem to work.

Don't trust me on this. Try it yourself. Use my techniques. Embarrass, humiliate, and otherwise electrocute yourself. I'm sure you'll end up just where I did, except maybe in a different city.

I was musing on my hard-won insights some weeks later when I found myself in the client's offices in Long Island, and I decided to stop in and see my old friend Sherry. We'd heard she still hadn't pulled the trigger on Lucifer but had been overruled in using the Nemesis by her boss, the SVP. It made sense: His agency was way too small to even begin to think about handling a serious Fortune 500 account. Maybe if he'd succeeded in luring more of the young analysts to join him, if his house party had worked like it was supposed to . . .

"You busy in here?" I asked Sherry.

She was sitting at her desk reading e-mail on a big flat screen and tapping a pen on a pad.

Tap tap tap.

She hesitated, then said hello.

"Have a second?" I asked her again and how could she say no? I was right there. I didn't even sit down on her guest chair. There was a small wooden crucifix glued onto her paper shredder, and she had a lovely gold cross around her neck.

"I was thinking," I started, "about the Gen Z project and I wanted to say we got it wrong. What I said was—you were there—we should embed in the social networks and get them to recommend and so on blah blah. You were there."

"Yup."

"But I've been thinking and I'm bothered by something. Can I sit down? Thanks—It occurred to me the whole thing may be wrong. Not just morally wrong—not like it's a good thing to get kids into debt before they even have an income really. But it's wrong for the market out there. People are changing. We see this with other clients. As consumers we're getting more—not just more *religious*, more *Catholic*—It's—what am I trying to say?"

She inclined her head slightly, mirroring my own motion.

"It's like we're—as a culture—we're getting *less cynical*. That's the best way to say it, I think. So I thought—Why not turn this Lucifer project around?"

"How?" she asked, studying my face.

"Instead of selling it to kids based on selfishness why not—why don't we sell it to parents as a tool. Make it a way to learn how to save. A vehicle for social responsibility and—here's an idea. Why don't we embed a savings account in the card instead of rewards points or cash-back. Or a—a college savings account. So there's a one point five percent cash-back put into a five twenty-nine in New York, or whatever. And it's only good for certain types of purchases."

"Like what?"

"Block out the SIC codes for entertainment, music, fast food—or maybe let the parents choose. Make it the card that only buys clothes and books and—and education—and doesn't work on—"

"On sin," she said.

"Exactly. That's the thought. Anyway—I know you didn't ask me. But I wanted to get that out there."

I stood up, trying to keep this seeming casual. The Navy SEALs might call it simply matching the weapon to the target.

"Yes, thanks," she said, "that's very interesting. An interesting twist."

"Let me know if you'd like to talk more about it."

She nodded. "Give me a call next week, let's talk more. It's a really neat idea."

As I left Sherry's office, I realized I had been surprised. Not that she liked the idea; I knew it was a good one. I was genuinely surprised by how great it felt to be a nice guy again, to consider something other than my year-end bonus.

I hadn't seen that coming.

• • •

I've heard there are no coincidences in life—only probabilities we don't understand.

As I stepped onto the elevator, I ran right into one of those probabilities.

"Marty," said the Nemesis, dressed in a shabby two-button pinstripe and worn-out black oxfords.

"Hello."

There were packs of people on the ride with us, and professional services people never—but *never*—speak on the elevator, because you do not know who's listening. Million-dollar accounts have been lost because of a stupid comment on an elevator. So we put our reunion on hold for fifty floors. During the ride, I couldn't help but notice my old friend looked a mite scrawnier than usual; probably he couldn't afford to hit the steroid dealership as often as he used to.

We walked out of the building together and started waving for our cabs.

"Where you working these days?" I asked him.

"Here and there. You?"

"Still at the agency."

"Sorry you guys lost Lucifer. Nice try."

"Sorry your company went under so fast. My condolences."

"Who told you that?" he asked, sharply.

"Well—Jaime and Roger came back last week. So we sort of figured."

He tried to edge in front of me, but I kept blocking him off, then he'd step in front of me and so on, as we did a silly dance with waving arms down the street toward the Chipotle's restaurant.

"What's next for you," I asked him, "direct mail?"

That was about as low as it gets—and I almost regretted my tone when I saw the hurt in his eyes. Almost. But then a cab started slowing in front of us and I rammed my forearm like a subway turnstile across his chest.

"That's my cab," he moaned, "you can get the next one."

"Not quite," I said—and jumped in, slamming the door behind me and locking it.

The Nemesis said something then I didn't quite hear, but I like to think it was that beautiful little word we all secretly long for but none of us hears nearly enough. The word that proved I'd learned a thing or two from my journey after all.

"Asshole!"

Acknowledgments

An Asshole no longer, I would like to gratefully acknowledge the support of the following people: Chae and Paul Kihn, Kathy Douglass, Jim Meddick, Mark Fefer, Mike Rubiner, Kim Cummings, Kate Taylor, Miriam Silverman, and all my friends on the "Fastbreak" morning crew, particularly Glenn G.

Special thanks to the team at Writers House: Simon Lipskar, for encouraging my pitch and coming up with the title; Dan Lazar, for great agenting and for saving this project at a critical point; Maja Nikolic, Jane Berentson, and Josh Gentzler.

Much love to Broadway Books: my dream editor Becky Cole, Brianne Ramagosa, Hallie Falquet, Julie Sills, Ellen Folan, and Rex Bonomelli. And to the true talent on the Left Coast: Paula Weinstein and Jeffrey Levine at Spring Creek, Zeke Steiner at Brillstein Grey, and the incredible Kassie Evashevski.

About the Author

Martin Kihn is an Emmy Award–nominated former writer for MTV's *Pop-Up Video* and the author of *House of Lies.* He has worked at *Spy, Forbes,* and *New York,* and his articles have appeared in *The New York Times, GQ, Details,* and *Cosmopolitan.* He lives in New York City.